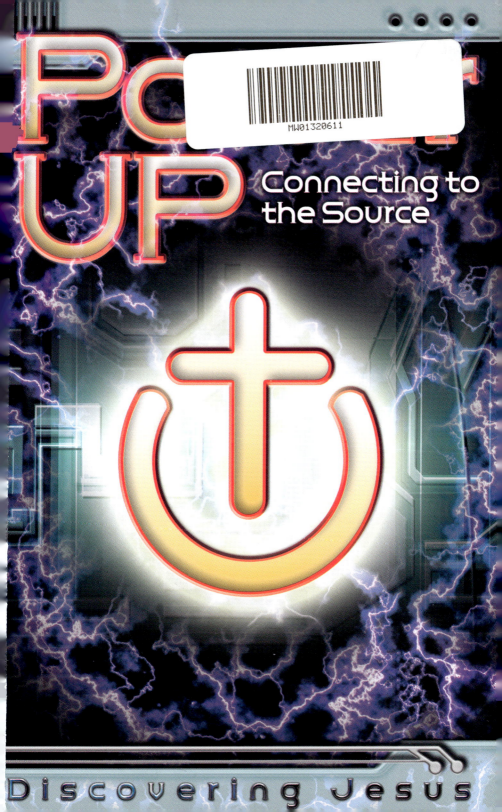

Conter
Connecting to the Source

5 ... Don't Worry; Be Happy!
6 ... This Is Boring!
7 ... I Know How You Feel
8 ... Pressure Points
9 ... Truth and Consequences
10 ... Safe at Home
11 ... Ready or Not!
12 ... Play to Win!
13 ... No One Is a Reject
14 ... Body Language
15 ... Friends: The Sequel
16 ... The Trust Factor
17 ... Reality Check
18 ... I Doubt It
19 ... Old School
20 ... Make Some Noise

Xtra Stuff

96 ... Maps
98 ... Answers
101 ... Discovering the Bible
104 ... Read the Bible in a Year

Xtra *Special* Stuff

117 ... Surge Protectors
122 ... The Bridge

Discovering Jesus

- 21 ... One Single Person
- 22 ... He's Here!
- 24 ... The Great Escape
- 25 ... Safe at Home!
- 27 ... Deleting & Saving
- 29 ... Downloading
- 29 ... Pressure Points – The Test
- 30 ... Friends: The Sequel
- 32 ... Make Some Noise
- 33 ... Something's Going Down
- 35 ... Reborn
- 36 ... I Know How You Feel
- 39 ... Listen to Me – Do It!
- 40 ... Work & Pray
- 42 ... The Calling
- 43 ... Truth and Consequences
- 45 ... Don't Worry; Be Happy
- 47 ... Radical Change Ahead
- 48 ... The Trust Factor
- 52 ... Point of Desperation
- 53 ... You're the Man!
- 55 ... Bright Lights & Strange Visitors
- 57 ... Call 911!
- 59 ... Play to Win!
- 60 ... 70 X 7
- 64 ... Mud Pies Revisited
- 66 ... Kids Are Welcome!
- 67 ... Rich Man, Poor Man
- 68 ... Body Language
- 70 ... Looking Good
- 73 ... Old School
- 75 ... Welcome Home!
- 78 ... Reality Check
- 80 ... Farewell
- 84 ... Friendship Denied
- 86 ... No One Is a Reject
- 90 ... Ready or Not!
- 93 ... I Doubt It!

Connecting to the Source

Power Up!

God is a source of power and strength for any and every situation you face. School is sometimes tough. You may love your parents but maybe you don't always understand them. They may not always understand you either. Your friends are up and down; hot and cold.

Everywhere you turn the media tempts you to think a certain way, like certain things and act a certain way. Let's be honest, what you see on TV and hear in music sounds like fun or looks pretty exciting.

Where do you find the power and wisdom to know what to do, and when? Sounds like you need to **Power Up** with God's Word. Get plugged in and get ready for the surge. It's just what you need!

Don't Worry; Be Happy!

Mark 4:35-41
See how Jesus dealt with this on page 45

Do you ever worry about stuff? Stuff you can control and stuff you can't?

Worry is when you think of the worst possible thing that can happen and focus on it. Faith is different than worry—faith is when you think of the best possible thing that can happen when God is involved. Imagine this: You're entering the lunchroom around noon and the possibilities for what can happen next are endless. Will you fetch your food then trip and spill it all? Will you look for somewhere to sit and find yourself sitting alone? Will you sit down with a group, strike up a conversation, and have the best lunch of your life? Who knows? But you can choose to believe that God will help you with lunchtime and make the most of it. Try it and see. Jesus has experience making lunchtime better!

This Is Boring!

"This is so boring! I am totally not into this."

Why do we get bored? Instead of enjoying what we are presently doing we think there is something more exciting we could be doing. Ever sit in class and think about riding your bike, playing ball, going to the mall, playing video games or just hanging with your friends? We have all wished we were doing something different. It's true—some stuff really is boring! But, if you try harder some of what you are presently studying, learning, reading or hearing could interest you more. I'm sitting in class; I'm supposed to be learning, and that can be fun if I am willing to make the best of it. I can't always be doing something different so I might as well enjoy what is happening and try to make the best of the situation.

Matthew 10:1-4
See how Jesus dealt with this on page 42

I Know How You Feel

Mark 4:35-41
See how Jesus dealt with this on page 36

Have you ever wondered where feelings come from?

Sometimes I feel happy and other times sad. Sometimes I feel courageous and other times full of fear. Sometimes I feel excited; yet other times I feel depressed. Feelings can change quickly and easily. I may feel sad if someone doesn't speak to me in the hall at school. I may be happy because I received a gift or I may just feel good for no particular reason at all. I may not always be able to choose how I feel but I can choose how I react to things that happen. Even though I may feel sad that doesn't mean I have to be rude or hard to get along with. Have you ever been around someone who has been sad or hurt so he treats others rudely? Your feelings shouldn't control choices or actions. With God's help you can choose how you act—no matter how you feel. God knows how we feel and He can help us make right choices in our actions.

Pressure Points

I have a test tomorrow...
Mom says take out the trash...

I have to read 10 pages in health... Dad says my room looks like a mess... My friends say I don't have to listen to my parents... I think I'm going to explode! Who do I listen to and how do I handle all this stuff people want from me? My parents want me to be the perfect child, my teacher wants me to be the perfect student and my friends want me to be the coolest friend. Sometimes I feel like I can't make anybody happy.

Excellent! It is impossible to make everyone happy. So what do I do next? Understand that you are not going to be a perfect student, child or friend. Be the best person you can be and you will honor your parents, friends and teachers. You might get to a point where you feel pressured to do something you can't or shouldn't do. Talk to your parents and talk to God about the pressure you are feeling. They'll help you and love you through the pressure.

Matthew 4:1-11
See how Jesus dealt with this on page 29

Truth and Consequences

Have you ever been tempted to cheat on a test?

Matthew 5-7
See how Jesus dealt with this on page 43

Why would anyone cheat on a test? DUH! You cheat on a test so you won't fail. But even if you pass the test, you still fail. Okay, now you are completely confused. If you cheat on a test because you didn't learn the material on the test, you have failed—the whole point of tests is to see what you have learned or not learned. You see, not being honest has consequences (bad stuff). Sometimes we think if we don't get caught then what is the harm? Understand, there still may be consequences.

Get this, you tell your parents you don't have homework so you can play video games. They don't question you so you think you got away with the lie. The next day the teacher has a quiz and you fail. Your parents get your report card and discover your grades are not what they expected. Your grades suffered because instead of telling the truth you lied and didn't do your homework. Busted! Jesus tells us that when we say "Yes" or when we say "No" those answers need to be the truth. Nuff said!

Safe at Home

"Parents just don't understand.

They are trying to ruin my life. They forget what it's like to be a kid." Okay, maybe parents don't completely understand but have you ever given any thought to what it's like to be a parent? It's a tough job. In fact parents and kids could learn a lot about each other if they could switch places for even one day. Ever seen the movie "Freaky Friday," where the mother and daughter's bodies are switched for a day? Both learned more respect for each other.

Home is a great place to be when parents and children have respect for each other—but without respect, home can be a war zone. Respect for parents means we won't blow our cool when they say "No." Parents usually have pretty good reasons for saying no. You ask your parents if you can have a friend stay over on a school night—they say "No." This is where respect comes in. Your parents explain that if your friend spends the night you probably won't get enough sleep; but your friend can spend the night on the weekend. Makes sense, so don't argue. God says honoring your father and mother will make life a lot smoother. I vote for smooth.

Luke 2:40-52
See how Jesus dealt with this on page 25

John 20:1-18
See how Jesus dealt with this on page 90

Tomorrow is coming.

Will the boy I like give me the time of day? Will the two girls who sit beside me in health make fun of me again? Will I get to talk to my parents about all that is happening in my life?

So much about the future is unknown and uncertain and may even cause us to experience fear. We sometimes fear stuff we can't control. Here's a news flash for you. A lot of stuff in your life and mine is out of our control. So how do I handle my fears? One way is through trust—trust that you have prepared enough for tomorrow's test and if you haven't, study some more. Trust that if you treat others kindly, they'll be kind to you. Trust that if you keep talking to your parents they'll listen and care about what you're saying. There is no guarantee! These situations may not go the way you want them to because you can't control another person's actions— you can only control your own. But if you make an effort to do what is right and trust God, He will help you respond to situations today and God will help you face whatever tomorrow brings.

Play to Win!

I hate losing!

I don't like to lose an argument. I don't like to lose at sports. I don't like to lose when I'm playing video games. I hate losing. I like winning. So what's wrong with that? Good question. It's easy to fall into the trap of believing that winning is everything, but it isn't. There's nothing wrong with competing hard and trying to win. Yet, if we will do anything to win, including cheating, name-calling or hurting another person's feelings, we have carried winning too far. If I yell at my teammates because they made a mistake, trash talk the opposing team, or get angry and stay that way because we lost, I'm probably too wrapped up in winning. So why even compete? Playing to win is okay when we learn teamwork. Playing to win is okay when we learn to work hard to get to a goal. Playing to win is okay when we simply understand that people are more important than wins. So play the game hard, work with the rest of the team, and if you lose don't let it rock your world. There will be other opportunities to play and to win. Some people say, "Everybody loves a winner." But God loves us whether we win or lose.

Mark 9:30-43
See how Jesus dealt with this on page 59

No One is a Reject

I was picked last for the dodge ball game and the science project. I was even picked last by the math teacher to answer a question. Sometimes I feel like a reject—like no one wants me around. Is it me? Am I really a reject? NO! No one is a reject. You may experience rejection—everyone does—but that doesn't mean you're a reject. There is stuff you do well. Maybe you're good at math, science, sports, music, dance, computers or any number of other things. You are special...you have special talents. God values you and loves you more than you could ever know. It's important to remember that whether you're chosen first or last—you are not a reject. You are important to God!

John 20:1-18
See how Jesus dealt with this on page 86

Body Language

I look in the mirror and sometimes I think I look fat,

or my nose looks too big or I wish my hair were a different color. Is there anyone else who struggles with how they look? Have you ever heard someone say, "Looks aren't everything"? Yeah, I know what you're thinking—that was probably written by somebody beautiful. It may be true but somehow it doesn't make me feel a lot better.

Luke 10:1-54
See how Jesus dealt with this on page 68

The truth is that every person is shaped just a little different and one shape or look is no better than another. The writer of Psalms says, "I praise you God for I am fearfully and wonderfully made." We were made by God to be who we are. We may be large or small; thick or thin; have dark, light, or even red hair; we may have large or small hands or feet; and our skin might be light or dark but we are special to God. Sometimes we worry too much about what's on the outside instead of focusing on what's on the inside. Do our actions reflect love, kindness and goodness? Because that is true beauty.

Friends; The Sequel

Who doesn't want or need friends?

But it seems like every time I make a good friend someone else comes along that she'd rather hang out with and she's gone. Sometimes the friends I make can't be trusted. I share my feelings or tell her secrets and she shares my secret with someone else and now, all of sudden, people are making fun of me. How do I know who to trust and who to be friends with? Why is it the people I want to be friends with don't always want to be my friends? How can I be a friend finder and keeper?

John 1:35-51
See how Jesus dealt with this on page 30

Begin by thinking about the qualities you want in a friend. Trust, kindness, fairness, forgiveness are just a few of the qualities that are important in good friendships. If you want to have good friends you can begin by being a good friend. Start by taking the first step. Meet people, ask questions so that you get to know them, and eventually you will find someone with common interests—and it will click. When you find this person, be the best friend you can be and you'll make a friend for life. Jesus says that good friendships are made when we care about people. Take the risk and eventually you will have a friend you can count on.

The Trust Factor

What is your fear factor?

What one fear do you have that you just can't overcome? Are you afraid of the dark, snakes, bugs, scary movies, strangers, or something bigger, like your parents getting a divorce or even death? How do you deal with fear? First of all it is not a bad thing to be afraid. Fear sometimes keeps us safe. Fear of being hit by a car can cause us to look both ways before crossing the street. Fear of burning your hand keeps a person from playing with fire. But if we let fear control us or keep us from doing what we know we should do, then fear is bad.

If you ask God for help with your fears, He can help you overcome them. But in order to receive God's help we have to trust. Trust means I'm going to depend on God to help me know when my fear can keep me from danger, or when my fear is just getting in the way of living life to the fullest. God, help us increase our trust factor and decrease our fear factor so we can have life!

Matthew 14:13-23
See how Jesus dealt with this on page 48

Reality Check

John 20:1-18
See how Jesus dealt with this on page 78

Have you ever worn a mask and pretended you were somebody else?

Although it's fun to pretend, there are some people who try to be anyone but who they really are. You've seen it. A girl or boy wants to be popular so she or he takes up swearing in order to gain the approval of friends. Or a certain guy wants to impress a certain girl so he lies about or exaggerates what he can or can't do. Why? To make himself look better than he thinks he is.

We try to be like people that we feel do something better than we do. But God doesn't want us to be a copy of someone else. He wants us to be the best "us" we can be. Do you realize that no two people have exactly the same color eyes or the exact same fingerprints? You are unique and that is exactly the way God wants you to be. So be you, be real, be unique, even a dead fish can go with the flow.

I Doubt It!

Magicians are fun to watch—

it's fun trying to figure out how they do their magic. They have an elephant on stage and then they make it disappear. Was the elephant really there? Did the magician really make it disappear? I doubt it. My doubt comes from my understanding that what the magician is doing is called an illusion. He is tricking us into thinking the elephant was really there or he is tricking us into thinking he really made it disappear. Sometimes we doubt what we are seeing or hearing is real. It's okay to doubt—sometimes we all do. But there is one event that we can be sure really happened—2000 years ago a man who was dead came back to life. His name was Jesus. Many people thought it was a trick but Jesus' coming back to life was no illusion. In fact over 500 people saw Jesus after God raised Him from the dead. Many of these witnesses saw Jesus die and therefore were amazed that He was now alive. Believe it or not, Jesus is alive! No doubt about it!

Luke 24:36-48
See how Jesus dealt with this on page 93

Old School

I feel like a square peg in a round world.

I dread going to school because when I get there everyone is in their little groups and I don't fit in any of them. I have tried everything. I have changed my style by dressing differently. I have tried to be interested in the things some of them are interested in. I have tried being nice but nothing seems to work. What do I do next?

First of all be you! You'll eventually find a group of friends who will accept you for who you are. Keep trying. Believe it or not, there are students at your school who will share your interests and value your friendship. Developing friendships takes time and once you have formed relationships with one or two students, you will be included in their circles. Also, look for friends who have similar priorities. Some groups you won't want to fit into—others might influence you in ways that might not benefit you. Ask God to help you find friends with whom you can be yourself. As "Old School" as that may sound I think it is good advice.

Luke 14:7-24
See how Jesus dealt with this on page 73

Make Some Noise

Matthew 4: 1-11
See how Jesus dealt with this on page 32

It's Friday night and you're hanging with some of your friends playing video games and listening to music. What are you listening to—is the music upbeat—something to move to? Is the music slow and somber—something to chill to? How do you decide what music you listen to? The reality is we don't always decide for a specific reason—we simply go with the flow. The music is on so we listen to whatever plays on the radio. You play a CD because lots of your friends are listening to it. You sing with a song because you hear it on the radio. You listen to an artist because you like the video.

Do you agree with the words in the songs? How do you feel when you hear the song? If your parents heard the song would they approve of you listening to it? Music is influential—it can influence your emotions, your thinking, and even your actions. Make a decision about the noise you listen to. When you listen to music, choose lyrics that are going to influence you in positive ways. You have a choice of where music moves you—be moved in the right direction.

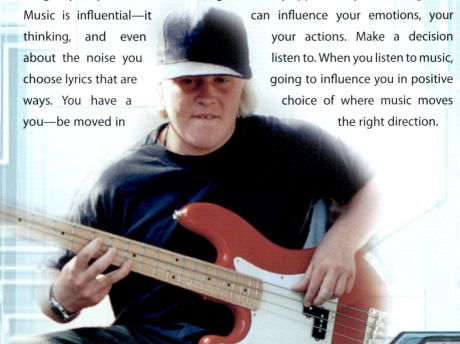

One Single Person —Jesus Christ!

He was born in a little known town to a young woman from a family living in poverty.

He grew up in another small town where He worked in a carpenter's shop until He was thirty; then for three years He was a traveling preacher.

He never had a family or owned a home. He never set foot inside a big city. He never traveled more than two hundred miles from the place He was born. He never wrote a book, attended college, or held public office. He did none of the things that usually come with greatness (in the eyes of the world).

While He was still a young man the tide of popular opinion turned against Him. His friends deserted Him. He was turned over to His enemies and went through the sham of a trial. He was nailed to a cross between two guilty thieves, and while He was dying, His executioners gambled for the only piece of property He had—His coat. When He was dead He was taken down and placed in a borrowed grave.

Twenty centuries (over 2,000 years) have come and gone, and today He is the central figure for much of the human race—our calendars are dated from His birth. We celebrate His birth and His resurrection on two of the most important holidays that exist. All the armies that ever marched and all the navies that ever sailed; all the legislatures that ever met and all the kings that ever reigned—put together—have not affected the life of men and women on this earth as powerfully as this **One Single Person—Jesus Christ!**

[Revised from "One Solitary Life," attributed to James A. Francis (1864-1928)]

He's Here!

Luke 2:1-39

The Roman emperor ordered a census to be taken which meant everyone had to enroll in the town from which their family had come—no one dared disobey his command. Soon travelers were going in every direction—Joseph and Mary headed for Bethlehem since they were both descendants of David's family.

From Nazareth a caravan of people started southward, the road leading through Samaria and over the hills to Jerusalem. From there Joseph and Mary went further south to Bethlehem. Some of their caravan stopped in cities along the way, while others joined them.

Surge Protector:

Glory to God in the heavenly heights, and peace to all men and women on earth who please him. Luke 2:14

When they reached Bethlehem it was crowded with people and Joseph couldn't find an empty room anywhere. The journey from Nazareth had been long and hard. Mary was very tired and wanted a place to rest! Joseph could find only the stable of the inn—that's where Baby Jesus was born. Mary wrapped him in soft blankets, called swaddling clothes, and laid him in a manger.

Shepherds were camping out in the fields near Bethlehem, guarding their flocks that night. Suddenly God's angel stood among them and a great light blazed around them—the glory of the Lord! The shepherds were terrified. Why was an angel hovering above them?

The angel said, "Don't be afraid. I have great news! I'm here to make an announcement that will be important to you and everyone all over the world for years to come. A Savior, the promised Messiah, has been born in Bethlehem—you'll find him in a manger."

What fantastic news! A chorus of angels sang, "Glory to God in the highest, and peace to all men and women on earth who please him." After the angels left the light faded into the still darkness of the night.

POWER SURGE

True or False or Who Knows?

1. Jesus was born on December 25th. **T F W**
2. Jesus was born in a stable. **T F W**
3. Gabriel is the angel who visited the shepherds. **T F W**
4. Joseph & Mary traveled to Bethlehem on a donkey. **T F W**
5. The "manger" is a wooden hay storage bin. **T F W**
6. The shepherds were told to look for a star. **T F W**
7. The angels sang "My Sweet Lord." **T F W**
8. There was snow that first Christmas. **T F W**
9. Baby Jesus cried. **T F W**
10. An angel told Joseph to take Mary to Bethlemen. **T F W**

See page 98 for answers

The shepherds all started talking at once, "Let's hurry to Bethlehem and see for ourselves what the Lord has revealed to us."

They left the sheep in the field and ran to Bethlehem where they found Mary, Joseph, and the infant Savior in a stable. Kneeling before the manger, they worshiped the little baby who lay quietly sleeping on the hay.

The shepherds told Mary and Joseph, "An angel of the Lord told us the news and a choir of angels sang praise to God." On the way back to their sheep they told everyone they met about the angel's visit and the Savior's birth.

When the baby was eight days old, Joseph and Mary named him Jesus, the name the angel had chosen long before Jesus' birth. The name Jesus means *salvation*.

According to Jewish law each family had to make an offering to God for their first baby boy. Rich people gave a lamb; poor people, two young pigeons or doves. When Jesus was 40 days old, Joseph and Mary took him to the temple in Jerusalem and gave two young pigeons to the Lord—it was all they could afford.

Simeon was led by God's Holy Spirit to go to the temple. God had promised him, "You won't die until you have seen the Savior." When Joseph and Mary brought Baby Jesus to the temple, God's Spirit revealed to Simeon that this child was the promised Savior.

Simeon hurried to meet Mary and took the baby in his arms. "Now may God let me go in peace; I have seen with my own eyes the salvation he has sent." Mary and Joseph were speechless!

Anna was very old, a woman who had served God faithfully all her life; in fact, she spent every day and night worshiping in the temple. When she saw Jesus she started praising God and told all the people around her about this Promised Child.

Mary never forgot what Simeon and Anna said about Jesus, and she especially didn't forget the shepherds' story. She thought about these strange things and wondered how her son, Jesus, would become the Savior of the world.

Reload

Anna – spent every waking hour praying and worshiping in the temple—for 84 years!

Month Jesus was born – possibly in September since sheep were generally out in the fields from March – November.

The Great Escape

Matthew 2

Wise men who studied the stars lived East of Judea. One night they discovered a new star—a signal from God that Christ had been born.

These wise men feared God and wanted to see this child who was to be the Savior of the world. They quickly packed their bags, along with expensive gifts for the newborn king, and set off to find him and to worship him as their Savior.

They traveled many days across the desert to Judea, then hurried to Jerusalem thinking they would find this wonderful child in the most beautiful and famous city.

When Herod heard about strangers riding into his city and asking lots of questions, he was very upset; in fact, most of Jerusalem was disturbed at the thought of a newborn king. What did it mean? Herod called the chief priests and religious leaders together and demanded, "Where is the Christ to be born?"

They remembered what the prophet had written long ago and answered, "The Savior is to be born in Bethlehem, and he is to rule his people."

Now Herod was even more upset. What if this newborn king planned to take away his throne? Secretly, he called the wise men and asked, "When did you see this star?" When they told him he said, "Go to Bethlehem and find the young child—look everywhere—when you find him, let me know so I can join you and worship him."

While they were in the city the wise men couldn't see the star but once they got outside the city gates they saw the bright star again, the one they had seen in the east country. They were relieved and excited! God must be leading them to Jesus.

POWER SURGE

1. The wise men stopped in Jerusalem to ask where they could find the King of the Jews. Why do you think they stopped there?

2. It turns out they actually took a detour. Jesus wasn't in Jerusalem. Have you ever had to take a detour? Have you ever been lost?

3. After the detour the wise men found the star again—waiting to guide them to Jesus. Have you ever asked advice from the wrong people instead of asking your pastor, Sunday school teacher or youth leader? How often do you check the Bible and ask Jesus for directions?

4. The wise men were excited when they found Jesus—so excited they gave Him gifts. Have you "found Jesus?" Were you so excited you told others about Him? What "gifts" have you given Jesus?

At Bethlehem the star stopped—finally, they had found the newborn king! They fell to their knees worshiping him. Then they gave him expensive gifts—gold, frankincense and myrrh.

Before the wise men left Bethlehem, God warned them in a dream not to go back to Herod, so they took another route back to their own country.

Not long after that God's angel told Joseph in a dream, "Get up and take the young child and his mother and escape to Egypt. Stay there until further notice—Herod will look for Jesus and try to kill him." Joseph, Mary and Jesus escaped from Bethlehem during the night, traveling to the country of Egypt.

Herod waited a long time for the wise men to return but they never came. They must have guessed why he had been so eager to see Jesus—Herod was furious! He sent soldiers to kill every boy two years old or less in Bethlehem and the surrounding area. Surely this would get rid of Jesus!

But Jesus was safe in Egypt. After Herod died God's angel told Joseph, "Get up, take the child and his mother and go back home."

They started back to Bethlehem, but when they arrived in Judea, Joseph was once again directed in a dream to go to the hills of Galilee. They settled in Nazareth and Joseph opened his carpentry shop.

Reload
1. The wise men were NOT kings, but astrologers. They did NOT visit Jesus on the night of His birth.
2. Jesus was probably 12–18 months old when the wise men saw him.
3. The Bible does NOT say there were three kings from the Orient.

Safe at Home!
Luke 2:40-52

When Jesus was a little boy he loved to watch his daddy work, and to play with the shavings that fell from Joseph's bench. Of course Jesus liked to run and play outdoors with his friends too.

Nazareth, Jesus' hometown, was nearly seventy miles from Jerusalem. The people couldn't go every week to worship God in Jerusalem; instead, they built a synagogue (church) in Nazareth where they heard the reading of books written by Moses and the prophets.

When Jesus was old enough to go to school, Mary and Joseph sent him to the synagogue where boys learned to read and write. They studied the psalms and the writings of Moses and the prophets. Just like other boys, Jesus memorized many scripture verses—no one had a Bible of his own.

One spring morning a group left Nazareth for the Feast of the Passover at Jerusalem—Joseph and Mary had gone every year since their return from Egypt. But the feast would be different for them this year; they were taking Jesus for the first time since he was twelve; in fact, now he would be going every year.

As the company moved slowly down the road people from other cities and villages joined them. At Jerusalem they met people from all over the land—it was so exciting! Jesus' eyes must have gotten really big when he saw the beautiful temple!

Jesus began to understand that God was his Father—that he must work with God—each day at the temple he listened to the chief priests and religious leaders and asked them questions.

After the feast the people of Nazareth started home. Mary didn't see Jesus but she thought he was with their friends and relatives. Evening came and still Mary didn't see Jesus; she and Joseph began to search for him. All through the company they asked, "Have you seen Jesus?" Always the answer was the same—no one had seen him that day. Now Mary and Joseph were really worried and headed back to Jerusalem hunting for Jesus.

On the third day they found him—not playing with other boys in the streets or learning to swim in the Pool of Siloam. Jesus was at the temple with the wise teachers, listening to them and asking questions. In fact, he had surprised the teachers in the temple, asking questions they couldn't answer.

Mary was really surprised to find Jesus there! She said, "Son, why did you stay here when we were all starting for home? Your father and I have been worried sick! We've looked everywhere for you."

Surge Protector:

Unscramble the words to find your protector.

SSJEU WREG NI

_____ ____ __

DMSIWO DAN

_____ ___

RATSTEU NAD NI

_____, ___ __

VORAF TWIH ODG

_____ ____ ___

DAN ENM

___ ___.   Luke 2:52

See page 98 for answers

Jesus answered, "Why did you look for me? Didn't you know that I would be at my Father's house?" Mary didn't understand—what did Jesus mean?

As the years passed Jesus grew to be a wonderful young man. He learned to explain the Scriptures and to talk with God. By helping Joseph with his work Jesus also became a carpenter, and when Joseph died, Jesus supported Mary and his brothers and sisters. His kind, thoughtful ways won him many friends. Jesus lived at home until he was about thirty years old.

POWER SURGE

1. Jesus was lost! Did you ever get lost? Was your mother or dad frantic when they found you? Were you scared?

Reload

1. Jesus grew up in Nazareth—He lived on the wrong side of the tracks.
2. This is the only story of Jesus as a boy.

Deleting & Saving

Matthew 3:1-12; Mark 1:3-8; Luke 3:2-20; John 1:15-28

When John was about 30 years old he left home and went all over the hill country of Judea preaching, "Repent, for the kingdom of heaven is at hand." Instead of going to the cities to preach God's message, John stayed in the country near the Jordan River. (See map on page 96.)

People came from all over to hear him speak. It had been over 400 years since the great prophets had spoken God's words to the people. No wonder they were anxious to hear John!

When people arrived to hear this strange desert preacher, they saw a man dressed in rough clothes made of camel's hair, with a leather belt around his waist. Because he spent all his time preaching in the country, his food was dried locusts and wild honey (Yuk!).

Many who heard John preach repented of their sins. Some criticized him, but all were impressed. News of this strange preacher spread like wildfire to the farthest corners of the country. Everywhere people wondered, "Who is this man?"

The religious leaders at Jerusalem sent priests and Levites to ask John, "Who are you?" John said, "I am not the Christ."

"Are you Elijah?" they asked. When John said he wasn't, they wanted to know, "Are you a prophet?" Again John's answer was no. Finally, the priests and Levites asked, "Then who are you? Tell us so we'll know how to answer the people who sent us."

To this John said, "I am the voice of one crying in the wilderness, 'Make straight the way of the Lord.'" The priests and Levites had another question. "Why do you baptize people if you are not Christ, or Elijah or a prophet?"

"I baptize with water," John explained, "but there is someone coming whose shoes I'm not even worthy to untie. He'll baptize you with the Holy Spirit, changing you from the inside out."

In the crowds John preached to there were all kinds of people—usually a few Pharisees and Sadducees, the religious rulers of the Jewish nation. They seemed to be very religious, but in their hearts, many of them were proud and sinful. They thought they were more religious and better than other people.

One time some of them came to John to be baptized and he said to them, "Who has warned you evil men to run from God's anger? You won't be ready to enter God's kingdom."

Those who believed John's preaching and repented of their sins asked him, "What should we do now?"

He answered, "The person who has two coats should give one to the man who has none. If someone has more food than he needs he should share with those who are hungry."

The tax collectors listened closely—they wanted to know what they should do. John told them, "Don't ask for more tax money than you're supposed to."

Soldiers also wondered what they should do since they had repented of their sins. "Don't abuse anyone or lie about anyone, and be content with your salary."

In the Jordan River John baptized those who confessed their sins. Because of that people called him "John the Baptist."

POWER SURGE

1. Don't you just love getting mail addressed to you? John was God's message to the people of that day.
2. People went to hear John because he spoke with power. Who would you go listen to?
3. What needs to be deleted from your life? What needs to be saved?

Downloading

Matthew 3:13-16; Mark 1:9-11; Luke 3:21-22; John 1:29-34

Jesus was 30 when he left Nazareth and went to the Jordan River where John preached and baptized the people. When John saw Jesus in the crowd he called, "This is the Lamb of God that takes away the sin of the world. He is greater than I could ever hope to be."

But Jesus hadn't come to be introduced to the people; he wanted to be baptized. John said, "Why do you want to be baptized by me? You're much greater than I am." John felt unworthy to baptize the Son of God.

Jesus answered, "I have to be baptized because it's God's plan—baptize me now." So John took Jesus in the river and baptized him there.

When the two were coming out of the water, a strange thing happened. The heavens opened up and the Spirit of God came down in the form of a dove and a voice from heaven said, "This is my Son, whom I love, and I am very pleased with him."

POWER SURGE

1. What would you say if...?
   - Shaq asked you to shoot his free throws
   - Mia Hamm asked you to kick a goal for her
   - Mark McGuire asked you to take his turn at bat
   - Stacie Orrico asked you to sing a solo in her place
2. How do you think John the Baptist felt when Jesus asked John to baptize him?
3. Have you been baptized?

Pressure Points – The Test

Matthew 4:1-11; Mark 1:12-13; Luke 4:1-14

After Jesus' baptism, the Spirit of God led him into the wilderness. Jesus knew God had great work for him to do—now he spent days thinking and praying about it.

After 40 days in the wilderness, the tempter (the devil) came to Jesus. Because he knew Jesus was weak and hungry, he said, "If you are the Son of God, turn these stones into loaves of bread."

Even though Jesus was very hungry, he refused. He would not use God's great power just to please himself. Instead, he trusted his heavenly Father to care for his needs. To the devil he said; "It is written. 'Man shall not live by bread alone; but by every word of God.'"

When this temptation failed, the devil tried another. Taking Jesus to the roof of the temple he said, "If you expect people to believe you are really God's Son; you have to prove it. Jump off the roof and trust God to protect you from getting hurt. Since he has placed you in the care of angels, they will catch you so you won't even stub your toe on a stone."

> **POWER SURGE**
>
> 1. Do you believe the devil is real? Why or why not?
> 2. Have you ever been tested, tempted to do things that were wrong? How did you handle the test? Did you fail or succeed?
> 3. What 3 things did the devil tempt Jesus with? How did Jesus respond to the devil?

Satan tempted Jesus with an easy way to get followers. Even though Satan had quoted scripture, Jesus didn't do stupid things. He knew the Scriptures taught a person should not do foolish things and then expect God's angels to help him. Jesus quoted Deuteronomy to the devil: "Don't you dare test the Lord your God."

Finally, on a high mountain, the devil showed Jesus all the kingdoms of the world. "These great kingdoms are mine;" the tempter said, "and I can give them to anyone I choose. They're yours—lock, stock and barrel. Just go down on your knees and worship me."

Jesus did not weaken. He answered, *"Beat it, Satan!"* He backed his rebuke with a third quotation from Deuteronomy: "Worship the Lord your God, and only him. *Serve him with absolute single-heartedness.*"

At last, Satan left Jesus alone; and angels came from heaven to care for Jesus' needs. He had won a great victory over the devil. Now he was ready to do his Father's work.

Friends: The Sequel

John 1:35-51

Many people believed the message John preached. With new eagerness, they waited for the coming of the King from heaven. They could hardly wait to hear that their King had arrived! In their hearts they believed he would set up a kingdom like David's, and the Jewish people would be favored.

One day John the Baptist saw Jesus walking along the road near the river when he cried out, "Behold the Lamb of God!"

Two of John's disciples had heard him say so many great things about Jesus they turned and followed him. When Jesus saw the two men coming after him, he asked, "What do you want?"

They answered, "Master, where do you live?"

"Come and see for yourself," Jesus said. He took the two with him and they talked all day.

Never had they heard a man speak as Jesus did! Andrew, one of the two, got so excited at what he heard he ran to find his brother—Simon needed to hear this! Both Andrew and Simon believed John the Baptist was a prophet of God. They listened to him often and followed him wherever he went.

Already Andrew was sure he had found a teacher even greater than John. When Andrew found Simon, he called out, "Come with me, we have found the Messiah!" So the two hurried back to Jesus.

When Jesus saw the brothers, he looked at Simon and said, "You are Simon, son of John; from now on you will be called Peter" (which means "Rock").

Simon was surprised! How did Jesus know his name? Jesus seemed to know all about him. As Simon listened, he too believed that Jesus was the Christ, and was just as eager to follow Jesus as was Andrew.

The next day Jesus started back to his home in Galilee. With him were his three new friends. As they walked along they met a man named Philip who lived in the same town as Peter and Andrew.

To Philip Jesus said, "Follow me." And Philip did.

As Philip walked with Jesus and the other three he marveled at the wise words Jesus spoke; surely this was the promised Savior and king. Philip was so excited he ran to find his friend Nathanael, and told him, "We have found the one Moses and the prophets wrote about, Jesus of Nazareth."

Because Nathanael knew the Scriptures well, he remembered the prophet had written that the king of the Jews would be born in Bethlehem. He said, "Nazareth?

POWER SURGE

1. Jesus knew Simon's name before they were introduced. He knows you too! How do you feel about that?
2. Jesus saw Nathanael sitting under a fig tree before they had ever met. Do you believe Jesus knows where you are all the time? Why or why not?
3. John's gospel is the only one where Nathanael's name appears. What is he called in the other 3 gospels?

You've got to be kidding."

Philip didn't waste a minute trying to convince his friend. Instead he said, "Come and see for yourself."

When Jesus saw Nathanael coming he said, "There's a real Israelite, not a false bone in his body!"

Nathanael was astonished. "Where did you get that idea? You don't know me," he said.

"One day, long before Philip called you here," Jesus said, "I saw you under the fig tree."

How could Jesus have known where he was and what he was doing? At once Nathanael believed that Jesus came from God. With joy he exclaimed, "Master, you are the Son of God! You are the King of Israel!"

Jesus said, "You've become a believer just because I said I saw you sitting under a fig tree one day? You haven't seen anything yet!"

Make Some Noise

John 2:1-11

A family in Cana of Galilee gave a feast. One of the family was getting married and had invited lots people to the wedding. Among the guests were Jesus, his mother, and his followers.

The wedding feast lasted several days. Perhaps the people were poor, or maybe they hadn't expected so many friends to come, but the feast was not over and the wine was all gone.

When Jesus' mother found out about this, she called her son aside. "They have no more wine," she explained. Wouldn't he help their friends at a time like this?

Mary called the servants. Pointing to Jesus, she said, "Do whatever he tells you."

And Jesus told them, "Fill the pots with water."

So the servants filled the huge jars to the brim. Then Jesus said, "Pour out some and take it to the governor of the feast."

Again, they obeyed. Instead of water, wine came out of the great stone jars. They were really surprised! Quickly they carried some to the governor of the feast, for he had to taste everything before it was served to the guests.

The governor took the wine without knowing what had happened. When he tasted it, he was surprised that this was much better than the wine that had already been served.

At once the governor called the bridegroom and told him, "At other wedding feasts the best wine is served first, but you have kept the best until the last."

This was Jesus' first miracle, the first glimpse of his glory. He had helped people who were in need and his disciples put their faith in him and marveled at what he had done. Surely no man could do such miracles!

POWER SURGE

True or False?

1. This is the first miracle Jesus performed. **T F**
2. Jesus turned grape juice into wine **T F**
3. The people throwing the party asked Him for money to buy more wine. **T F**
4. His mother didn't think Jesus could do miracles. **T F**
5. The party lasted several days. **T F**
6. The custom of the day was to save the best for last. **T F**
7. Jesus performed this miracle to show off his powers. **T F**
8. Jesus performed this miracle to help some friends. **T F**

See page 98 for answers

Something's Going Down

John 2:13-25

When it was time for the Passover, people from every part of the land went up to Jerusalem to keep the feast. Among those who went were Jesus and his friends—Andrew, Simon, Philip, and Nathanael.

When Jesus entered the temple court, he found it crowded, noisy and busy. Nothing about it made a person feel like praying—it looked more like a busy mall than a house of prayer. Men had brought live oxen, sheep and doves into the temple to sell for sacrifices.

These animals only added to the noise and confusion.

POWER SURGE

Something's going down: you walk into your church on Sunday and find vendors selling CDs, DVDs, T-shirts and jewelry; guys are standing at every door, and you can't go any farther until you pay $85.00—and it has to be paid in silver dollars—no paper money or quarters—just 85 silver dollars. There is a booth where you can get change, but that will cost you another $25 dollars.

1. What pops into your mind?
2. How do you feel about what's happening?
3. What can you do about this? What comes to mind?

Reload
- A half shekel is equal to a dime in the US.
- It took 2 days of working to earn a half shekel.
- If they had "unclean" money from another country, not a half shekel, they had to pay another half shekel to exchange it for "clean" money.
- After exchanging their money, they then had to pay big shekels for an animal to offer as a sacrifice.

The loan sharks were there in full strength too. Every Jew over twenty years old had to give a piece of silver money called a half shekel to the priests. This money was used for sacrifices and for the temple.

Those who came from distant countries brought the kind of money used in their homeland. Since half shekels were the only coins the priests would take, all other coins had to be changed for half shekels to pay the priests. On top of that, every person had to pay to have his money changed into temple coins.

Jesus was so angry when he saw people having a carnival in God's house! Taking small strips of leather, he tied them together and made a whip. With the whip he drove out all the animals and their keepers. Then he upset the loan sharks' tables, spilling coins left and right. To those who sold doves he said, "Get your things out of here! Stop turning my Father's house into a shopping mall."

Many were angry at Jesus for doing this. They asked, "What miraculous sign can you show to prove you have a right to do all this?"

Jesus knew they would not believe him even if he showed them a sign. He answered, "Tear down this temple and in three days I'll put it back together." Jesus meant the temple of his body. He knew the Jews would help to kill him. Then in three days he would rise from the dead.

The Jews didn't understand. They thought Jesus meant the great temple Herod had rebuilt. They were indignant: "It took forty-six years to build this temple and you say you can rebuild it in three days?" Shaking their heads doubtfully, they walked away.

During the time Jesus was in Jerusalem for the feast, he began to teach the people and to do miracles among them. Many believed in him when they heard his words and saw the great works that no other man could do.

Reborn

John 3:1-21

One man who believed in Jesus was a leader among the Jews. He was Nicodemus, a rich Pharisee. Most of the Pharisees were very proud. They didn't believe that either John the Baptist or Jesus were teachers sent from God.

Nicodemus was not like other Pharisees. He heard Jesus teach the people who had come to worship at the Passover. "Surely Jesus is a great man," Nicodemus thought.

While other Pharisees were finding fault with Jesus, Nicodemus wanted to hear more of his teachings. One night he went to the house where Jesus stayed to talk with him.

Nicodemus said, "Master, we know you are a teacher straight from God. No man could do the miracles you do unless God was with him."

Jesus wanted Nicodemus to know about the kingdom of God. He said. "You're absolutely right. Unless a person is born again, from above; it's impossible to see the kingdom of God."

Nicodemus was puzzled. He asked; "How can a man be born after he is grown up? Can he become a tiny baby again?"

Jesus didn't mean that a man would be born again in body but in heart. He said, "Unless a person is born of water and of the Spirit, he or she cannot enter the kingdom of God. When you look at a baby, it's just that: a body you can look at and touch. But the person who takes shape inside the body is formed by something

Surge Protector:

Fill in the blanks using the vowels to finish the words. —John 3:17 (THE MESSAGE)

G _ d   d _ dn't   g _   t _
_ ll   th _   tr _ _ bl _   _ f
s _ nd _ ng   h _ s   S _ n
m _ r _ ly   t _   p _ _ nt   _ n
_ cc _ s _ ng   f _ ng _ r,
t _ ll _ ng   th _   w _ rld
h _ w   b _ d   _ t   w _ s.
H _   c _ m _   t _   h _ lp,
t _   p _ t   th _   w _ rld
r _ ght   _ g _ _ n.

See page 98 for answers

POWER SURGE

1. How do you feel about the fact that God loved you so much He willingly gave His one and only Son to be tortured and to die on the cross, so you could have a whole and lasting life?

2. Have you accepted God's free gift of His Son? Have you accepted His help?

3. If not, please ask someone to pray with you. If you need help in finding someone to talk with, contact us at powerup@warnerpress.org.

Reload

Nicodemus was part of the "in crowd," but he was not a happy camper. He came to Jesus with feelings of guilt and loneliness. Jesus loved him, right where he was, and offered him new life—life everlasting.

you can't see and touch—the Spirit—and becomes a living Spirit. Don't be surprised when I say that you must be born again, from above. The wind blows—you hear it rustling in the trees and you see what it does—yet you don't see the wind itself. You can't tell where it comes from or where it goes. That is the way it is with those who are born again, from above."

Nicodemus thought about Jesus' words. No one could see the Spirit. Yet a person whose heart was changed, born again, would act as if he or she had the Spirit of God in his or her heart.

Finally Jesus said tenderly, *"This is how much God loved the world: He gave his Son, his one and only Son. And this is why: so that no one need be destroyed; by believing in him, anyone can have a whole and lasting life. God didn't go to all the trouble of sending his Son merely to point an accusing finger, telling the world how bad it was. He came to help, to put the world right again."*

I Know How You Feel

John 4:1-43

Jesus decided to return to Galilee, so he and his disciples took the shorter road that led through Samaria. Not many Jews went this way because they hated the Samaritans and the Samaritans didn't like the Jews! Although both worshiped God, the Samaritans had built a temple in their own country instead of going to Jerusalem to worship.

In many ways Jesus was not like most other Jews—for one thing, he didn't hate the Samaritans. He knew that God loved the people of every land. He couldn't just avoid the Samaritans—he knew their spiritual hunger—even if they didn't.

When they had traveled as far as the little city of Sychar, Jesus was worn out and sat down to rest by a well Jacob had dug hundreds of years before. The disciples left him to rest and went into the city to buy food.

Surge Protector:

True worshipers will worship the Father in Spirit and in truth.   John 4:23 (NIV)

At noon a woman from Sychar came to get water. She knew at a glance that the strange man sitting there was a Jew. Since they wouldn't give Samaritans the time of day, she passed by him and lowered her water jug into the deep well. When the jug was full, she pulled it up again.

Just as the woman was ready to start back to the city, Jesus said, "Would you give me a drink of water?"

The woman was so surprised at his request that she said, "Since you're a Jew, why do you ask a Samaritan woman for a drink? You know the Jews have nothing to do with the Samaritans."

Jesus replied, "If you knew our generous God and who asks you for a drink, you would be asking me to give you living water."

The woman didn't understand and said, "Sir, this well is deep and you don't have anything to draw water with; how could you give me living water? Are you greater than Jacob who gave us this well?"

"Anyone who drinks this water will be thirsty again and again," Jesus answered. "Anyone who drinks the water I give will never be thirsty again—it's like an artesian spring, gushing fountains of life."

Now the woman was really interested. She didn't know the living water was Jesus' free gift of salvation to all people. So she said, "Sir, give me this water so I won't have to come here to get water any more."

Jesus told the woman things about herself she thought no one knew. He told her all the wrongs she had done.

The woman wondered how this stranger could know so much about her. Then she decided, "Sir, I believe you are a prophet." Because she didn't want to be reminded of her sins, she tried to start an argument about religion. She said, "We Samaritans worship here, but your people say we should go to Jerusalem to worship."

Jesus didn't argue, instead, he explained that God planned to bring salvation through the Jews. "God doesn't care what you're called or where you worship," he said, "It's who you are and the way you live that count before God. He is looking for those who

> **POWER SURGE**
>
> 1. Is there anyone you really dislike? Is there someone who has let you know they don't like you? How do you handle these feelings? How should you handle these feelings in light of this story?
> 2. What would you think or do if someone walked up to you and started telling you everything you'd ever done that was bad?
> 3. What did the Samaritan woman do? What did Jesus do for her?

are simply and honestly themselves before him in their worship. God is Spirit, and those who worship him must do so from their spirits, in adoration."

The woman had never heard such wonderful words. She said, "I know the Messiah is coming from God. When he arrives he'll tell us everything."

The woman was really surprised when she heard Jesus say, "I am he! You don't have to wait any longer." Before she could ask him more the disciples returned with food and were shocked to see Jesus speaking to "that" woman. She could tell by the looks on their faces what the disciples were thinking—she took off, forgetting her water jug. She ran to tell her friends about this wonderful stranger.

The disciples offered Jesus food. "Teacher, eat something," they said.

Jesus refused. "I have food to eat you know nothing about."

The disciples whispered to one another, "Did someone bring him food while we were away?"

Jesus knew their question so he answered, "The food that keeps me going is doing the will of my Father who sent me."

Back in the city, the woman ran through the streets telling the people about Jesus. "Come see a man who told me all the things I ever did—he knows me inside and out," she said. "Do you think he is the Christ?" The people were so curious they decided to go see for themselves, so they went back to Jacob's well with her.

Jesus talked with the Samaritans about the things of God. They invited him to stay and teach them more, so Jesus stayed two more days teaching the people of Sychar and many believed. They said to the woman who first met Jesus at the well, "Now we believe—not just because of what you told us, but because we heard it for ourselves. We know this man is the Christ, the Savior of the world."

Jesus took his disciples and went on to Nazareth.

Reload

- Jesus performed NO miracles for the Samaritans.
- The Samaritans were considered "outsiders."
- Because of Jesus, the Samaritans were finally included; they belonged.

Listen to Me – Do It!

Luke 5:1-11

Jesus' disciples went back to their work as fishermen when they returned to Capernaum. One day Jesus was standing on the seashore where Peter, Andrew, James and John were scrubbing their nets.

Many people had seen Jesus leave the city so they followed him, crowding around, trying to hear what Jesus had to say!

Jesus climbed into Peter's boat and asked him to move out from shore. Sitting there Jesus began to teach the people. After Jesus finished speaking he told Peter, "Put out into deep water and let your nets out for a catch."

Peter replied, "Master, we've been fishing all night and haven't caught a minnow, but if you say so, we'll try again."

Peter and Andrew rowed out from shore and let down their nets one more time. The nets hit the water and the fish hit the nets! It became so heavy they couldn't pull the net out of the water and it began to break. They waved to their partners in the other boat to come help. Never had they seen so many fish! Soon both boats were full of fish—so full they began to sink.

When Peter saw this he fell to his knees before Jesus and said, "Leave me, Lord! I'm a sinner." All the fishermen were overwhelmed by the catch of fish!

Jesus had no intention of leaving them. He answered, "Don't be afraid. From now on you'll be fishing for men and women."

POWER SURGE

1. Do you like to fish? What's the biggest fish you ever caught?
2. When you go fishing do you get tired just sitting there, waiting for the fish to jump on your hook?
3. What kind of bait do you use? Squiggly worms or jumping crickets?
4. Ever had your parents or teacher tell you to do something you thought was really stupid, but when you did it, it was really awesome?
5. Jesus helped his friends by doing what?
6. Did they want to listen? What happened when they did listen to Him?

Work & Pray

Mark 1:16-38

As Jesus walked by the Sea of Galilee he saw Andrew and Peter fishing. He called out to them, *"Come with me! I'll show you how to fish for men and women instead of fish."* They immediately dropped everything and followed him—no questions asked.

As the three walked along the shore, they saw two other fishermen—the brothers, James and John—mending their nets. Jesus **made the same offer** to them as he had to Andrew and Peter. James and John immediately left their ship to follow Jesus.

With the four fishermen, Jesus returned to Capernaum. On the Sabbath they went to the synagogue—the meeting place—where many people came to hear Jesus. When he spoke, they felt as if God was talking to them.

In the crowd was a man who had a very bad spirit. The bad spirit made the man yell, "Leave us alone! What are you doing here, Jesus of Nazareth? I know you are the Holy One of God. You want to destroy us!"

Jesus said to the bad spirit, "Quiet! *Come out of him!*" The bad spirit *shook the man violently and came out of him with a shriek.*

The people were so surprised! They'd never seen anything like this! They asked one another, *"What is this? Some new teaching?* He gives orders to bad *spirits and they obey him!"*

Jesus and his friends went to Peter and Andrew's house where they learned that Peter's mother-in-law was sick with a fever. *Jesus took her hand, helped her up,* and the fever left instantly. She got up and made dinner for them.

For the Jews the Sabbath ended at sunset. After sunset nearly the whole town showed up outside Andrew and Peter's house, bringing family and friends who were sick. Jesus was glad to help the people—he healed many that night.

POWER SURGE

1. What would you do? Jesus asks you to leave your family, your home, your job, and your friends to follow Him all over the country.

2. If you were busy all day long and even late into the night and slept only a few hours, would you want to get up and pray? Or keep sleeping? Could your parents or friends even wake you up?!

3. Jesus was God's Son. He was special and had great powers, but He still found time to talk to His Father. Do you think He NEEDED to talk to God? Why? What did He get out of talking to God?

Jesus was very tired, but after sleeping only a few hours, he got up quietly and left the city. He found a place where he could be alone to talk with his heavenly Father. Jesus prayed for strength and help to accomplish his mission on earth.

When the sun came up more people showed up at Peters house, asking for Jesus. Peter and his friends didn't find Jesus at the house so they went to look for him and found him praying.

"Everyone's looking for you," they said.

Jesus answered, "Let's go somewhere else—to other cities—so I can preach there too; after all, that is why I'm here." So the disciples went with him to other cities in Galilee. Jesus taught in the synagogues and healed the sick—many believed in him.

Reload

In Matthew 6:9-13, Jesus teaches the disciples and us how we should pray.

Find a King James Version Bible and look up this scripture and fill in the blanks.

Use the words from the blanks and find them in the word search.

```
P A S C E T Y M O L W R B O T K M E
L A R Z A H G E F H I J E H L O F I
E J O D G I V E N O E V G E D T O W
D Y T X E N M A K I C A S I M A R H
O A B L R E M E S B I E V P Y Y G A
E R E S G I P O J Q U H T E R E I N
B O D A H L V E D I F E M A N I V T
J S E M S D O L A G W L X T G I E Y
O F I D A E L R A C N E V I L M O S
L A R I T W E K Y P T I S E P T L D
H E L A D O C V I E G E K T I R E O
E Y I M E L S Z A M E N A V E N W A
A T D O K L E R P W D T I H A R I F
G I V A C A T E F S I E T G Y E L A
E O B R E H N I D O J A V L B A L K
A P O W E R T E N E F I C T O S G E
F I Q U O A B G A R E V I L E D V E
S T E H S U T E K E P V N O M I A J
```

Our _____ which art in _____, _____ be thy _____. Thy _____ come. Thy _____ be done in _____, as it is in heaven. _____ us this day our _____ _____. And _____ us our debts, as we forgive our _____. And _____ us not into _____, but _____ us from _____: For _____ is the kingdom, and the _____, and the _____, for ever. _____.

See page 98 for answers

The Calling

Luke 6:12-16

Many people besides the four fishermen, Philip, Nathanael (called Bartholomew in Luke) and Matthew, followed Jesus. His stories and teaching were so interesting that many wanted to be his pupils or disciples, so they followed Jesus from one town to another.

Because Jesus knew his time was short he chose twelve men to train so they could help in his ministry. He wanted to send these men to places he had never gone—to teach and preach to people about God.

Jesus knew the hearts of all these men—he spent days with them, but he knew he needed God's help in choosing the Twelve. He slipped away quietly and climbed a mountain to pray. He prayed all night for wisdom, help and for strength to finish his work.

When morning came Jesus called his followers who were waiting in the valley and chose twelve of them to be his apostles. He chose Simon (whom he named Peter) and Andrew, his brother. Then he chose James and John, the brothers who had been partners with Simon and Andrew in the fishing business. Afterwards he chose Philip, Bartholomew, Matthew, Thomas, James, the son of Alphaeus; another Simon, called the Zealot; Judas, the son of James (also called Thaddaeus); and last of all Judas Iscariot who betrayed Jesus.

Jesus gave these twelve men the power to heal and told them to preach the kingdom of God. These twelve were called apostles—those who are sent out.

POWER SURGE

True or False?
1. Four fishermen were chosen T F
2. Matthew was a tax collector (IRS agent) T F
3. Peter & James were brothers T F
4. Philip was 1 of the 12 T F
5. There were 2 Simons in the group T F
6. Thomas doubted Jesus T F

Word Search
- ☐ Simon Peter, ☐ Andrew, ☐ James (son of Zebedee),
- ☐ John, ☐ Matthew, ☐ Philip, ☐ Thomas,
- ☐ Bartholomew, ☐ James (son of Alphaeus),
- ☐ Simon, ☐ Thaddaeus, ☐ Judias Iscariot

```
S P R A F B M E L G I K H A D
T H A D D E A U S J W C O J S
I O M U O F T M Q A O E N L I
B H I J R P T A N M I H E B T
L T P R S G H O W E R D N A O
O E C E A R E N F S T A J R D
D I L T O C W O E M I D E T P
E K U E T J S A B S E T C H E
M A H P S E T I N G A J I O F
S G W N A H E N S U R L E L M
N Y T O O S O L D A I B H O J
A F Y M Z M R I E P D Q E M C
W J A I I C E J G T W U N E S
E S E S B S L A D U F E J W R
L K P X E H M O K E J A M E S
```

See page 98 for answers

Truth and Consequences

Matthew 5-7

After Jesus had chosen his twelve disciples, he wanted to teach them how to do his work. Up the mountainside, they climbed. Then Jesus sat down and they got close to hear him. Many others crowded in to hear Jesus too.

Blessed (happy, joyful, satisfied inside) are…

- the poor in spirit: for theirs is the kingdom of heaven. *(When you're at the end of your rope, you think less of yourself and more of God.)*

- they that mourn: for they shall be comforted. (When you think you've lost the greatest things in your life God will embrace you—He is the best.)

- the meek, for they shall inherit the earth. *(When you're content with who you are, you'll find you have everything that can't be bought*—the most important inheritance you can have.)

- they which do hunger and thirst after righteousness: for they shall be filled. (When you have *a good appetite for God*, He'll be *the best meal you'll ever eat.*)

- they who show mercy to others, for mercy shall be shown to them. (When you care more about others, you'll *find yourselves cared for.)*

- they who have pure hearts, for they shall see God. (When your mind and heart are right, then you will see God all around you.)

- those who make peace among men, for they shall be called the children of God. *(When you show people how to cooperate instead of fight, you discover who you really are, and your place in God's family.)*

- they who are persecuted for the sake of righteousness; for theirs is the kingdom of heaven. *(When people put you down or tell lies about you, it means the truth is too close for comfort and they are uncomfortable.)*

POWER SURGE

dntas	sgvei	sheuo	nheis	ese	oogd	ddsee
tasl	threa	lasyt	dgoo	rwnhto	apdtmler	tilgh
saprie	htafre	neehav	ticy	tcaonn	ddhnie	lepope
drnue	wlob	utp	roldw	plam		

_____ _____ _____ _____ _____ _____ _____

_____ _____ _____ _____ _____ _____

_____ _____ _____ _____ _____ _____

_____ _____ _____ _____ _____ _____ _____

_____ _____

You are the _____ of the _____. But if the salt loses its saltiness, how can it be made _____ again? It is no longer _____ for anything, except to be _____ out and _____ by men. You are the _____ of the _____. A _____ on a hill _____ be _____. Neither do _____ light a _____ and put it _____ a _____. Instead they _____ it on its _____, and it _____ light to everyone in the _____. In the same way, let your light _____ before men, that they may _____ your _____ _____ and _____ your _____ in _____.

Matthew 5:13-16 (NIV)

See page 99 for answers

Rejoice, and be exceeding glad; for great is your reward in heaven. (*Be glad when that happens—cheer even—they don't like it, but I do! Heaven applauds. You're in good company—my witnesses have always gotten into this kind of trouble.*)

Jesus taught the disciples (and us) how Christians should live, how they (and we) should pray, how all of us should treat enemies and friends, how God loves and cares for all.

At the close of his sermon Jesus said, "If you live by my words you are like a smart man *who built his house on solid rock.* The *river flooded and a tornado hit* but the house stood strong—*fixed to the rock.*"

"But if you just read my words, even do *Bible studies*, but don't apply them to your life and live them, you are like a *stupid* man *who built his house on a sandy beach.* When a storm came in the waves got high, the house collapsed—like it was made of sticks."

When Jesus finished the people broke into applause and gave him a standing ovation! *They had never heard teaching like this before*—it was fantastic! The challenge was to live it—with God's help.

Reload

Man's Best Friend—a Tale of Love

Attributed to Watchman Nee

A new Christian who was very upset came to Watchman Nee and said, "No matter how much I pray, no matter how hard I try, I simply cannot seem to be faithful to the Lord."

Nee said to him, "Do you see this dog here? He is my dog. He is house-trained; he never makes a mess; he is obedient; he is a pure delight to me. Out in the kitchen I have a son, a baby son. He makes a mess, he throws his food around, he fouls his clothes, he is a total mess. But who is going to inherit my kingdom? Not my dog; my son is my heir. *You are Christ's heir because it is for you that He died.*"

Don't Worry; Be Happy

Luke 8:22-25

Jesus spent all day teaching. It was now evening and he said to his disciples, "Let's head for the other side of the lake." The disciples and Jesus all got in one boat, and some who saw them leave got into their own little boats and followed.

Suddenly, a bad storm came up that sent waves pouring into the boat, nearly sinking it. The disciples pulled at the oars with all their strength, but they were fighting a losing battle. If the boat broke to pieces they would be lost.

POWER SURGE

1. Are you more afraid of lightning or thunder?
2. Have you ever been out on a lake or the ocean in a storm? Were you scared? Did you get sick?
3. Do you think Jesus slept through the storm because He was so tired, or because He was at peace?

Several disciples were seasoned fishermen but they had never seen the sea rage like this before. They were completely helpless in the power of the storm. What should they do?

Jesus was so tired from teaching all day he had fallen asleep in the stern, his head resting on a cushion. The storm didn't bother him a bit.

At first the disciples didn't want to wake him, knowing how tired he was, but now that the boat was about to sink, they ran and woke him up. "Master, don't you care if we drown in this storm?"

Jesus stood up and spoke to the wind and the sea, *"Quiet! Settle down!"* At the sound of his voice *the wind ran out of breath and the sea became smooth as glass.*

Jesus looked at the frightened faces of his disciples and asked, *"Why are you such cowards? Don't you have any faith at all?"*

The disciples were amazed and asked each other, "Who is this man? Even the wind and the waves obey him!"

Surge Protector:

HET   ISIDCLESP   EOWK   MHI   DAN   ASDI

___   _____   ____   ___   ___   ____

OT MIH, "RCETAHE,   T'ODN OYU AREC

__ ___, "_____,   ___'_ ___ ____

FI   EW   WNROD?"   EH   OTG   PU,   BEUREDK

__ __ _____?" __ ___ __, _____

HET NWID NAD DAIS OT HET VASEW,

___ ____ ___ ____ __ ___ _____,

"TIQUE!   EB   LILTS!"   HENT   HET   DINW   DDIE

"_____! __ _____!" ____ ___ ____ ____

NOWD   DNA   TI   AWS   MLTECOPELY   MALC.

____   ___   __ ___   _____   ____.

MARK 4:38-39 (NIV)

See page 99 for answers

Radical Change Ahead

Luke 8:26-39

After Jesus stilled the storm, he and his disciples went ashore in the country of the Garasenes, *across the lake from Galilee*. Nearby was a cemetery where a wild man lived—a man separated from his family and friends—alone and lonely. No chains were strong enough to hold him. Night and day he wandered in this lonely place—without clothes, shrieking, and bloody from cutting himself with stones.

When the wild man saw Jesus, he ran, fell at Jesus' feet and worshiped him. The evil spirits that tortured him caused him to shout at Jesus, "What do you want with me, Jesus, Son of the Most High God? I beg you, don't torment me!"

Jesus knew the man could never be well as long as he was filled with evil spirits. Jesus said, "Come out of the man, you unclean spirit." Then he asked the man, "What is your name?"

The evil spirit replied, "My name is Legion, for we are many." The wild man was telling Jesus, "I am really sick. I don't even know who I am any more."

A herd of two thousand pigs was feeding on a hillside nearby. The evil spirits begged Jesus to let them go into the pigs.

"Go," Jesus answered.

The pigs went crazy and *stampeded over a cliff into the lake and drowned*. The servants taking care of the pigs were *scared to death* when they saw this! They ran to town to tell what had happened.

Soon a crowd of curious people gathered. They were surprised to see the wild man sitting at Jesus' feet, wearing clothes and acting perfectly fine—*in his right mind*.

POWER SURGE

1. Have you ever felt alone? Ever been lonely? Can you even imagine living like the wild man in this story?
2. Do you have a special friend who likes you just the way you are? Someone who allows you to be yourself? Who understands you?
3. Can you believe it! The people were more concerned about losing the pigs than they were about people being healed! What do you think about them?
4. How do you think people in your neighborhood or town would react if something like this happened today? Why?

Reload
- Legion means thousands. A Roman legion equaled 6,000 soldiers

The people were scared—what kind of man was Jesus? A whole herd of pigs had drowned because of him. The cost was too high! *They got together and asked Jesus to leave—too much change, too fast.* Bruce Larson writes it was as if they were saying, "We'd rather have a few crazies around than have our property destroyed. If that's the cost of healing, no thanks, we don't want it!"

Jesus and his disciples got in the boat, and the man who had been healed followed. He wanted to go with them, but Jesus said, "Go back to your home and tell your friends everything God has done for you."

The man gladly obeyed—going from city to city, telling people how much Jesus had done for him.

The Trust Factor

Matthew 14:13-23; Mark 6:30-46; Luke 9:10-17; John 6:1-15

The disciples returned, reporting to Jesus about the people they had healed and taught in Galilee. More and more people heard about Jesus and they came from everywhere to hear him and see him.

The people were so eager to hear Jesus and have their loved ones healed they followed him everywhere. He didn't have time to rest or even to eat so Jesus called the twelve disciples and said, "Let's get away to a quiet place where we can rest awhile."

They sailed to the other side of the sea but they didn't find much time to rest—the crowd had followed them to the other side. Perhaps the disciples were disappointed because the people had found them again, but Jesus looked at the people lovingly and sat down to teach them again and to heal the sick.

Late afternoon came but still the people stayed. They seemed to forget they couldn't find food or shelter in the desert. The disciples wanted Jesus to send the crowd away so they could find rooms *for the night and get a bite to eat. They were out in the middle of nowhere.*

But Jesus asked Philip, *"Where can we buy bread to feed this crowd?"*

Philip answered, "Two hundred dollars wouldn't buy enough bread *for each person to get a piece!"*

In this crowd were five thousand men besides all the women and children. When they left home they didn't know they would have to go so far to find Jesus.

A young boy heard Jesus and the disciples talking about what to do. He went up to Andrew, showed his lunch basket and offered to give the food to Jesus. Andrew took it to Jesus.

"How many loaves are there in the basket?" asked Jesus.

"Only five loaves of bread and two small fish," Andrew said. *"But that's not a drop in the bucket for a crowd like this!"*

"Bring it to me," Jesus replied. To the disciples he said, "Make the people sit down in groups of fifty and a hundred."

Jesus took the bread and fish, gave thanks, and broke the food into small pieces, then filled a basket for each disciple to pass among the hungry people.

When the crowd was full Jesus told the disciples, *"Gather the leftovers so nothing is wasted."* The disciples filled twelve large baskets with leftover bread.

The people were awed by this miracle. They wanted Jesus to become their king, but Jesus wouldn't allow it. He hadn't come to earth to set up an earthly kingdom, so he slipped off and went up the mountain to be alone.

POWER SURGE

1. If you had 500 people show up unexpectedly in your back yard for a picnic, what would you do?
    a. Borrow a charge card
    b. Order pizzas delivered
    c. Send out for chicken
    d. Run away from home
2. What would you think if you were one of the 5,000?
    a. I hate fish. I'm out of here!
    b. My friend invited me here and we didn't even make a hamburger run first!
    c. They're serving lunch? I hope they don't put onion on my hamburger!
    d. Ummm! Smells good! I'm hungry!

POWER SURGE

Unscramble the underlined words in the scripture, writing them on the blanks below.

After you've unscramble them, find these same words and circle them in the word search. Look forward, backward, up, and down.

12. And when the day <u>geban</u> to wear away, then came the <u>wevlet</u>, and said unto him, Send the <u>etultmiud</u> away, that they may go into the towns and <u>onrcuty</u> round about, and <u>ogled</u>, and get <u>tulvcias</u>: for we are here in a desert place.
13. But he said unto them, Give ye them to eat. And they said, We have no more but <u>evfi</u> loaves and two fishes; except we should go and buy <u>etma</u> for all this people.
14. For they were about five <u>huantosd</u> men. And he said to his disciples, Make them sit down by <u>teiffis</u> in a <u>ypocman</u>.
15. And they did so, and made them all sit down.
16. Then he took the five loaves and the two fishes, and looking up to <u>enevah</u>, he blessed them, and <u>karbe</u>, and gave to the disciples to set <u>eorbfe</u> the multitude.
17. And they did eat, and were all <u>lldife</u>: and there was taken up of <u>trmfagens</u> that remained to them twelve <u>tsabeks</u>.

Luke 9:12-17

_____ _____ _____ _____ _____

_____ _____ _____ _____ _____

_____ _____ _____ _____ _____

f	g	j	y	r	t	n	u	o	c	s
k	r	b	e	g	a	n	q	a	v	e
f	b	a	s	k	e	t	s	g	e	i
i	r	j	g	w	m	y	h	p	d	t
l	a	c	o	m	p	a	n	y	u	f
l	k	d	t	w	e	l	v	e	t	i
e	e	g	d	o	l	n	e	v	i	f
d	n	a	s	u	o	h	t	p	t	t
b	v	i	c	t	u	a	l	s	l	y
x	o	c	n	e	v	a	e	h	u	k
z	l	w	b	e	f	o	r	e	m	b

See page 99 for answers

Point of Desperation

Matthew 14:23-36; Mark 6:47-56; John 6:16-29

In the evening the disciples climbed into their boat and started rowing across the sea to Capernaum. Jesus was still on the mountain alone.

Surge Protector:
Don't be afraid; it is I. Mark 6:50

After dark a strong wind started blowing across the sea, beating against the boat. The disciples rowed like crazy but they didn't make much progress against the turbulent wind and waves that grew higher and higher, dashing against the boat.

The disciples were nearly worn out—they'd made little progress. Their strength was about gone and their nerves were raw. Truth is—they were scared! They probably remembered the time Jesus was with them and calmed the storm—if only he were with them now!

Jesus had prayed for several hours; in fact, it was between 3:00 and 6:00 A.M. when he decided the disciples were in desperate need of him. Jesus walked out across the water just as if it were land.

The disciples looked up and saw a person walking on the waves. They were in such a panic they almost missed him! Each of them thought he had seen a ghost—no man could walk on the water. They screamed and some started to jump in the sea.

When Jesus heard their screams he said, "Don't be afraid; it is I."

The voice sounded like Jesus but the disciples could hardly believe it was him. Finally, Peter called out, "Lord, if it's really you, tell me to come to you walking on the water."

He answered, *"Come ahead."*

Peter jumped over the side of the boat and started walking on the water to Jesus. The other disciples' mouths dropped open in amazement. Jesus had such great power!

When a strong wind blew against Peter he looked at the waves and began to sink. "Lord, save me!" he cried out.

Jesus reached down and grabbed Peter's hand. "You have such little faith; why did you doubt?" Jesus asked.

The two climbed into the boat and the wind stopped. Again, the disciples were astounded at the Lord's great power. They worshiped him, saying, "Surely you are the Son of God."

When morning came the crowd that had been with Jesus the day before went to find him again. They had seen the disciples leave in the only boat around but Jesus had stayed behind. They looked everywhere but couldn't find him. When some boats landed from Tiberias, they sailed across the Sea of Galilee to Capernaum in their search for Jesus.

Wherever Jesus went, in villages or cities or in the country, the people begged him to let the sick touch the hem of his robe—all who did were healed.

Surge Protector:

1. Are you afraid of storms? Why? Or why not?
2. Ever been in a bad storm out on the water?
3. Would you freak if you saw someone walking towards you in the middle of the ocean or even a big lake?
4. Would you jump out of the boat like Peter did? Why or why not?
5. If you did jump out, would you sink? Or would you stay on top?
6. Why do you suppose the disciples were so scared considering they had just seen Jesus feed over 5,000 people with 5 loaves of bread and 2 fish? DUH!
7. Why do you think Jesus let the disciples row in a storm for 6 hours before He went to help them?

You're the Man!

Matthew 16:13-28; Mark 8:27-9:1; Luke 9:18-27

Jesus and his disciples traveled north to the city of Caesarea Philippi. On the way he asked, "Who do people say I am?"

The disciples answered, "Some think you are John the Baptist, risen from the dead. Some say you are Elijah the prophet, come back to earth; and others say you are Jeremiah or another prophet who taught long ago."

Next Jesus asked, *"But what about you? Who do you say I am?"*

Boldly Peter answered, "You are the Christ, the Son of the living God."

Jesus rejoiced to hear this. At least his disciples understood who he was. But Jesus warned them not to tell anyone.

Then he talked about the troubles and sorrows that would come to him at Jerusalem. He would be arrested and cruelly treated. Because the *religious leaders, high priests and religious scholars* would try him and find him guilty, he would be killed. But, after three days, he would *be raised to life.*

The disciples just didn't get it. They thought Jesus was going to be their king soon and that each of them would have an important place in his kingdom. Why in the world would he talk about dying now?

Peter grabbed Jesus' arm in protest, then took Jesus aside and said, "These terrible things can't happen to you!"

Jesus turned and saw that his disciples were wondering what to believe. He rebuked Peter. "*Get behind me, Satan!*" he said. "*You have no idea how God works!*"

POWER SURGE

1. Who do YOU say Jesus is?
2. Do you believe Jesus is who He says He is? Why? Or why not?
3. Is it hard for you to follow Jesus?

It would have been a whole lot easier for Jesus if he could have set up a kingdom on earth—no humiliation, no beating, no pain and suffering, no hanging on a cross for hours until he suffocated and died. But that was not God's plan, and more than anything, Jesus wanted to do God's will—no matter what.

Later, Jesus called the people and his disciples around him and told them what it meant to be his follower. "If you want to follow me, you must *let me lead. You're not in the driver's seat; I am.* You must not be selfish and only take care of yourself. *What good would it do to get everything you want and lose you, the real you? What could you ever trade your soul for? If any of you are embarrassed over me and the way I'm leading you when you get around your friends, know that you'll be an even greater embarrassment to the Son of Man.*"

People were astounded at the things Jesus said!

Bright Lights & Strange Visitors

Matthew 17:1-13; Mark 9:2-13; Luke 9:28-36

Jesus took Peter, James and John with him on a long hard climb up a rough mountain slope near Caesarea Philippi. Jesus was going to spend time with his Father, praying, and wanted these three men to join him in prayer. They were used to rowing boats, but not to climbing mountains—Peter, James and John fell asleep.

When the disciples woke up they found Jesus praying: *His appearance changed from the inside out, right before their eyes. Sunlight poured from his face. His clothes were filled with light.*

The disciples could hardly believe their eyes when they saw their Master's glory! In astonishment, they watched as Moses and Elijah appeared and began talking to Jesus!

As the men were leaving, Peter said to Jesus, *"Lord, this is a great moment!* Let's build three monuments: one for you, one for Moses, and one for Elijah."

While Peter rambled on, a cloud appeared and surrounded them so that they were afraid, but *deeply aware of God.* A voice spoke out of the cloud: *"This is my Son, marked by my love, focus of my delight. Listen to him."*

The next minute the disciples were looking around, rubbing their eyes, seeing nothing but Jesus, only Jesus.

The next day as they climbed down the mountain, Jesus ordered them not to tell anyone about what had happened. Then he said, *"After the Son of Man rises from the dead, you're free to talk."* Still the disciples wondered why he talked about pain and death when he had been in the bright lights on the mountain.

POWER SURGE

True or False?

1. The disciples stayed awake all night praying with Jesus. **T F**
2. Jesus slept while the disciples prayed. **T F**
3. Jesus' appearance changed because He was struck by lightning. **T F**
4. The disciples really did see Elijah and Moses talking with Jesus. **T F**
5. It was God who spoke out of the cloud. **T F**

See page 99 for answers

POWER SURGE

Read this story of The Transfiguration in Matthew 17, fill in the blanks, and then finish the crossword puzzle.

Jesus took __6D__, __1A__, and __5D__ to the mountain with Him. Matthew 17:1

Jesus' face shone as the __11A__. Matthew 17:2

Jesus' raiment was white as the __4D__. Matthew 17:2

One of the two men from past history that talked with Jesus. __12D__ Matthew 17:3

A prophet from the past that talked with Jesus. __8D__ (New Testament spelling) Matthew 17:3

Peter wanted to build three of these. __7A__ Matthew 17:4

After the transfiguration, while Peter spoke, what overshadowed the group? __3A__ Matthew 17:5

God's voice said, "This is my beloved Son, in whom I am well pleased; __9A__ ye Him." Matthew 17:5

When the disciples heard God's voice, they were __10D__. Matthew 17:6

Jesus came over and touched the disciples and said, "__2D__, and be not afraid." Matthew 17:7

After Jesus reassured the disciples, they looked up and saw __5A__ only. Matthew 17:8

Jesus said to the disciples, "Tell the vision to no man, until the Son of man be __13A__ again from the dead." Matthew 17:9

See page 99 for answers

Call 911!

Matthew 17:14-21; Mark 9:14-29; Luke 9:37-43

Jesus and his three disciples left the Mount of Transfiguration and arrived in the valley where they found the other nine disciples surrounded by a huge crowd and religious teachers who were *cross-examining them*.

> **Surge Protector:**
> If you believe, anything can happen.
> Matthew 17:23

A man ran out of the crowd and fell at Jesus' feet. "Lord, my son *is possessed by a spirit that has robbed him of speech. It seizes him and throws him to the ground; then he foams at the mouth, grinds his teeth, and goes stiff as a board.* I brought him to your disciples, but they couldn't help."

Jesus was so disappointed that his disciples didn't have enough faith to heal the boy. "*What a generation! No sense of God! No focus to your lives!*" Jesus said, "*How many times do I have to go over these things*? How long shall I put up with you?" Turning to the troubled father, Jesus said, "Bring the boy to me."

As they brought the boy he had an attack. He fell to the ground, lay in the dust and foamed at the mouth.

"How long has your son been this way?" Jesus asked.

The father answered, "Ever since he was a little boy. Many times he has almost lost his life when these attacks threw him in the fire or into the river. If you can do anything, please, *have a heart* and help us."

Jesus knew the father didn't have much faith. "If you believe," Jesus told him, "*anything can happen.*"

Immediately the father cried, "I do believe; help me not to doubt!"

Jesus gave the bad spirit *its marching orders*: "*Dumb and deaf spirit, I command you—out of him and stay out!*" The boy was so quiet and pale people said, "He's dead."

Jesus stooped down, took the boy's hand and lifted him up. The boy stood on his own feet and walked to his father—completely well.

As soon as the disciples could be alone with Jesus, they asked, "Why weren't we able to heal the boy?"

"Because you didn't have enough faith; *you're not taking God seriously*," Jesus said. "You can't help people unless you live a life of prayer." And he talked to them about their need for faith in God.

POWER SURGE

1. Have you ever had to call 911? What happened? Were you scared?
2. Have you seen someone prayed for? Did they get better?
3. Have you ever been prayed for? How did you feel? What happened?
4. Why weren't the disciples able to help this boy when they prayed for him?

Directions: Use the code chart below to complete the sentences. Choose from the numbers on the left first, then add number on top. (for example: 35=Q).

	1	2	3	4	5	6
1	A	B	C	D	E	F
2	G	H	I	J	K	L
3	M	N	O	P	Q	R
4	S	T	U	V	W	X
5	Y	Z				

___ ___ ___ ___ ___ ___ ___ ___ ___ ___ ___ ___ ___ ___
31 23 36 11 13 26 15 41   33 16   24 15 41 43 41

___ ___ ___ ___ ___ ___ ___ ___ ___ ___ ___ ___ ___ ___
13 11 26 31 15 14 42 22 15 41 42 33 36 31

___ ___ ___ ___ ___ ___ ___ ___ ___ ___ ___ ___ ___
45 11 26 25 15 14 33 32 45 11 42 15 36

___ ___ ___ ___ ___ ___ ___ ___ ___ ___ ___ ___ ___
16 23 41 22 11 32 14 26 33 11 44 15 41

___ ___ ___ ___ ___ ___ ___ ___ ___ ___ ___
45 11 42 15 36 42 33 45 23 32 15

___ ___ ___ ___ ___ ___ ___ ___ ___ ___ ___ ___
42 45 33 12 26 23 32 14 31 15 32

___ ___ ___ ___ ___ ___ ___ ___ ___ ___ ___ ___ ___ ___
12 33 51 45 23 42 22 41 15 23 52 43 36 15 41

___ ___ ___ ___ ___ ___ ___ ___ ___ ___ ___ ___ ___ ___ ___ ___
26 11 36 21 15 13 11 42 13 22 33 16 16 23 41 22

See page 99 for answers

Play to Win!

Matthew 17:22-18:14; Mark 9:30-43; Luke 9:43-50

Leaving the north country Jesus and his disciples started back to Capernaum through Galilee—Jesus didn't want anyone to know where they were—He wanted time to teach his disciples. On the way Jesus told them, "The Son of man *is about to be betrayed to some people who want nothing to do with God.* They will kill him, but after three days he will rise, alive." The disciples didn't understand what he was saying, but were afraid to admit it.

As they walked along some of the disciples began to argue about who would be the "top dog" in Jesus' administration. They still thought Jesus would set up an earthly kingdom, like a corporation, and offer them well-paid, powerful positions.

When they reached Capernaum, Jesus took his disciples to a friend's house where they could have some privacy—few people knew about this secret hideaway.

One day when they went to town, a tax collector for the temple in Jerusalem stopped Peter and asked, "Doesn't your master pay taxes?"

"Yes, of course," Peter answered.

When Peter returned to the house Jesus told him, "*Go down to the lake, throw out your line, and pull in the first fish that bites. Open its mouth and you'll find a coin. Take it and give it to the tax men* for our taxes." Peter went fishing, found the piece of money in the fish's mouth just as Jesus had said, and paid the tax.

When all the disciples were together Jesus asked them, "What were you guys arguing about on the way?"

No one said a word. You could have heard a pin drop! They were too ashamed to say anything but Jesus already knew what they had been talking about. He sat them down and started another lesson, "If any of you wants to be first, he must be last and serve others."

Taking a little child in his arms, he said, "Unless you change and become like little children, you will never enter the kingdom of heaven. When you are humble like this child, then you are the greatest, and if you welcome a child like this in my name, you are welcoming me."

POWER SURGE

True or False

1. Jesus wanted everyone in Galilee to know he and his disciples were traveling through. They had a parade. T F
2. Peter found money for the tax collector in a bucket by the lake. T F
3. Peter, James and John argued about which of them was the greatest. T F

See page 99 for answers

1. How did the three feel when they realized Jesus knew they were the ones who were arguing, and what they were arguing about?
2. Have you ever argued about something really stupid? How did you feel? What did you do?

To show the disciples how important each person was, Jesus said, "If a man has a hundred sheep and one runs off, doesn't he leave the ninety-nine and go looking for the one that is lost? And if he finds it you know he is happier over that one than over the ninety-nine that didn't run away. Your heavenly Father feels the same way; he doesn't want to lose a single person."

Then John told Jesus some of them had seen a man healing people in Jesus' name. "We told him to stop doing that because he wasn't part of our group."

"Don't stop him," Jesus said. "If someone does a miracle in my name he's helping in my ministry." Jesus must have been discouraged that his disciples understood so little about him and his work.

70 x 7

Matthew 18:21-35

One day Peter asked Jesus, "Lord, how many times do I need to forgive a brother or sister who hurts me? Seven times?" (The law in those days was to forgive 3 times.)

Jesus replied, "Seven times only? How about seventy times seven!"

Peter nearly choked. Could he ever forgive that many times?

Jesus told Peter a story about a king whose servant owed him lots of money (10,000 talents – see **Reload** to find out how much that equals today!). The king called his servant and asked him to pay up, but he couldn't. So the king said, "Since you can't pay back the money you borrowed, I'm going to auction off you, your wife and your kids; plus, I'm selling everything you own. That way I'll get back at least some of the money you owe me."

The servant fell on his face, crying, and begged the king. "Please, be patient; give me a chance and I'll pay back every penny I owe!"

Because the king felt sorry for the man, he said, "I'll forgive all the debt, and you don't have to pay it back." (WOW!)

This servant was no sooner out the door when he met another poor servant who had borrowed only a few dollars from him (100 denarii – see **Reload** to find out how much that equals today!). He asked the man to pay it back, but the man couldn't. The servant got so angry he took the poor man by the throat and yelled, "Pay back what you borrowed or I'll have you thrown in jail!"

The poor man fell on his knees and pleaded, "Please, be patient with me, and I'll pay back every penny I owe."

But the king's servant wouldn't listen. Because the poor man didn't have any money, the king's servant had him thrown in jail.

When other servants of the king saw what had happened they were really upset and told the king everything.

The king was furious—he couldn't believe his servant had been so cruel! He quickly called the man into his office and read him the riot act. "You are so bad! I forgave all of your huge debt when you begged me. Couldn't you have forgiven the small debt your poor neighbor owed you—just like I forgave you? You're out of here, buddy, and headed for prison until you pay me back every cent you owe!"

When Jesus finished the story, he said to Peter, *"That's exactly what my Father in heaven is going to do to each one of you who doesn't forgive, unconditionally, anyone who asks for mercy."*

ABCs of FORGIVENESS

Forgiveness Means…
- **A**ccepting that we've been hurt and we're angry, BUT that holding a grudge is a waste of time and energy
- **B**eing FREE from hurt and anger, ready to get on with living
- **C**aring more about the PERSON(S) than about what he or she did to us
- **D**oing Acts of Kindness to/for the person(s) who hurt us
- **E**xperiencing God's forgiveness to us because we forgave others

POWER SURGE

1. What is the main teaching of this parable? On the lines below, write the letter that corresponds to the sign language above it.

____ ____ ____ ____ ____ ____ ____

2. How many times are we supposed to do that?
   _____

3. Do you have a hard time forgiving? Why? Or why not?
   _____
   _____

4. Does someone come to mind that you haven't forgiven? What will you do about that?
   _____
   _____

See page 99 for answer

Reload

- 10,000 talents equals $12 million dollars in US money today!
- 100 denarii equals $20 in US money today!
- Our debt to God is way beyond what we could ever pay!

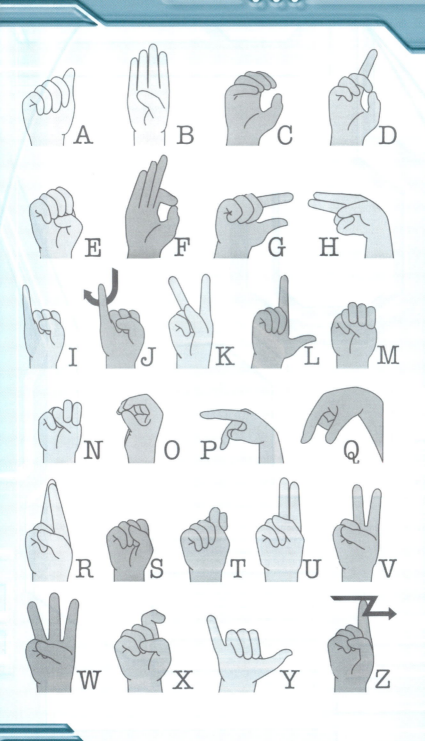

Mud Pies Revisited

John 9

One Sunday as Jesus left the temple, he saw a blind man begging beside the road. This man had been blind since birth and lived with his parents in Jerusalem.

The disciples had seen him before. They asked, "Lord, who sinned—this man or his parents—that caused him to be born blind?"

"You're asking the wrong question," Jesus said, *"You're looking for someone to blame. Look instead for what God can do."*

The disciples watched as Jesus stopped in front of the blind man, spit on the ground, and made some mud with his saliva. Jesus then rubbed it on the blind man's eyelids.

"Go wash in the pool of Siloam," Jesus told the poor man.

Without a word, the blind man got up, felt his way to the pool, washed the mud off his blind eyes, and immediately he could see! He ran home, yelling for all he was worth, "I can see! I can see!"

Everyone was surprised when he told what had happened! Some even asked, "Isn't this the man who used to sit and beg?" Some said, "It's him!" Others replied, "No, it just looks like him."

The man who had been blind settled the question by saying, "It is me!"

People really got excited when they heard that Jesus had opened the blind man's eyes. They gathered around him and asked, "What did he do to you? How did he open your eyes?"

The man told how Jesus mixed a little mud, rubbed it on his eyes and sent him to wash in the pool of Siloam. "I did what he said and then I could see," he said, with a big grin on his face.

"Where is this man?" the people asked. "I don't know," he answered.

The neighbors marched the once-blind man to the Pharisees, who grilled him over and over about how he could see. Finally they said, "This Jesus can't be from God because he doesn't keep the Sabbath."

Some people standing by said, "But how could a sinner do miracles?"

So they were divided. Some thought Jesus had the power of God; others thought he was playing tricks on those who believed him.

Turning back to the man who had been healed, the Pharisees asked, "What do you think about this man? It was your eyes he opened."

The man replied, "I believe he is a prophet."

Jesus' enemies were really upset over this miracle. They tried to find some way to prove it wasn't true—that the man had only pretended to be blind. They called his parents and questioned them, "Is this your son?" they asked. "Is he the one who was born blind? How do you explain the fact that now he can see?"

His parents were afraid since the leaders had already said that anyone who confessed Jesus as the Christ would be turned out of the synagogue. So, when asked to identify their son and tell how he was made to see, they answered, "He is our son and he was born blind, but that's all we know. Ask him. He can speak for himself."

POWER SURGE

1. Okay, how would you feel about having mud put on your face by someone you didn't know and couldn't even see?
2. Would you follow that person's instructions and go wash your face in a ditch?
3. Or would you think the person was a nut case and tell him or her to take a hike?
4. The man born blind—who now could see—was thrown out of the synagogue by religious leaders. Why? How would you respond to that kind of treatment?
5. Being able to see when he was born blind was fantastic, but an even greater miracle took place in his life? What was it?
6. Have you had that miracle, that healing in your life? Do you believe?

Jesus' enemies were getting really angry. They called the man born blind back a second time and asked, "What did Jesus do to you? How did he open your eyes?"

He said, "I told you already and you wouldn't listen. Why do you want to hear about it again? Do you want to become his disciples?" Wrong answer!

They jumped all over him. "We're disciples of Moses! We know God spoke to Moses but we have no idea where this man came from."

Now the man Jesus had healed said boldly, "I'm not believing this! You don't know where Jesus came from but he opened my eyes! We've been taught and we know that God does not listen to sinners—He listens to the man who does his will."

Nobody's ever heard of opening the eyes of a man born blind—ever. This man has to be of God or he couldn't do anything like that.

The leaders were really angry now because this man dared to try to question them, so they threw him out. He was no longer welcome at their worship.

When Jesus heard what had happened, he went to find the man and asked, "Do you believe in the Son of God?"

The man answered, "Who is he, sir? Tell me so I may believe."

Jesus said, "You're looking at him; he's speaking to you right now."

"Lord, I believe!" the man said, and worshiped him.

Kids Are Welcome!

Matthew 19:13-15; Mark 10:13-16

While Jesus was teaching the people, mothers kept bring their little children so Jesus could put his hands on the children and pray for them. It was the custom in those days for children to be touched and blessed by a great teacher after their first birthday.

When the disciples saw the mothers and heard the noise the children made they didn't like it. Jesus was too busy teaching and the noise was too distracting, the disciples thought. He didn't need to be bothered with little children when he had people to heal—that was much more important! The disciples were aggravated with the mothers and said, "You shouldn't bother Jesus with your squirming, squealing children. He has more important work to do."

The mothers were really disappointed! They wanted—no, needed to see Jesus and talk to him. Some of them had walked a long way, carrying their children.

Just then, Jesus saw the mothers and called the children to him. He was upset with the disciples—they just didn't get it! He had just talked to them *(see Play to Win)* about being humble like a little child, and welcoming children. Weren't they paying attention? Looking at the disciples he said, "Don't you dare keep these little ones from me! Listen: *Unless you accept* God's kingdom like a little child *you'll never get in.*" Then Jesus picked up the children, held them in his arms, and blessed them.

Jesus knew children would gladly trust him and believe him—that many times they would lead older people to believe in him too. He knew their hearts were tender and quick to respond to his love.

POWER SURGE

1. Do you ever feel that people at school, at church or at home are too busy for you? How does that happen?
2. Do you have a special place (not your house) where you always feel welcome? Where or what is it?
3. What does *welcome* feel like to you?
4. How do you feel about Jesus after reading this true story?

Rich Man, Poor Man

Matthew 19:16-30; Mark 10:17-31

One day a rich, young, powerful man came running to meet Jesus—he was eager to talk to this man, and he was used to getting what he wanted. Although this young man wore expensive clothing, he still had respect for authority. Kneeling down in the dust in front of Jesus he said, "Good Teacher, what do I need to do to get eternal life?"

"Why do you call me good?" asked Jesus. "Only God is good. You know the commandments; 'Do not kill,' 'Do not steal,' 'Do not tell lies,' 'Honor your father and mother.'"

"Yes, I know the commandments of Moses," the young man replied, "and I have kept them since I was a child. But something's missing; I feel empty. Tell me, please, what is it?"

Reload

Rich man, poor man, beggar man, thief...none can enter by their own merit or need, but all can be saved by the gift of God.

—David L. McKenna

Jesus liked this guy! Fact is—he loved him! And he really wanted to help him! So, Jesus spoke the truth in love, "You're missing one thing. Go home, sell all you

POWER SURGE

Can you imagine! This guy had Jesus' full attention! He had great prospects for the future with Jesus as one of His disciples, and ultimately, Heaven. But he walked away, gave up a sure thing for some money and a few "things."

1. Is there any "thing" you would find hard to give up?
2. Do you ever feel like there's something missing in your life?

have and give your money to the poor—then you'll have riches in heaven. After that, come back and follow me."

Bummer! That is NOT what the young man was expecting to hear! Gloom and doom fell on his face when he heard those words! He just wasn't willing to give up all he had worked so hard for—he made a very bad choice and walked away!

Jesus watched him go away. Then turning to the disciples he said, "It is so hard for rich people to enter the kingdom of God!"

The young man loved his money and his things more than he loved God. He would never be happy because his heart wasn't right with God. He would always feel something was lacking, something clouding his hope of life in heaven.

Body Language

Luke 10:25-37

A lawyer came to Jesus and tried to trick him with a question. He asked, "Teacher, what do I have do to get eternal life?"

Jesus wasn't fooled! He was aware that this man knew the 10 Commandments very well. So, instead of answering the question, he asked the lawyer, "What is written in the commandments? How do you interpret them?"

The lawyer replied, "Moses wrote that we should 'love the Lord your God with all your heart, and with all your soul, and with all your strength, and with all your mind.' And he wrote that we should 'love your neighbor as yourself.' "

"Good answer!" Jesus said. "Do it and you'll live."

But the lawyer had another question, "Who's my neighbor?"

Surge Protector:

Thou shalt __6__ the __14__ thy __7__ with all thy __9__, and with all thy __2__, and with all thy __4__.

This is the __10__ and __8__ __1__.

And the __12__ is like unto it, Thou shalt __14__ thy __5__ as __11__.

On these __15__ commandments hang all the __3__ and the __13__.

Matthew 22:37-40

See page 100 for answers

Jesus answered him by telling a story about the Good Samaritan. "One day a man was traveling down the road from Jerusalem to Jericho, minding his own business. Robbers jumped him, took his money, tore off his clothes, beat him, and left him for dead beside the road.

"Soon a priest came along and saw the man lying there, nearly dead, but instead of stopping to help, he crossed to the other side of the road, as if he didn't even see him. Next, a Levite (a religious person) came by and saw the man lying beside the road, but he didn't even give him a second look. He hurried on, leaving the poor man to die."

POWER SURGE

1. Loving ourselves is pretty easy. We don't have to think about it, we just do it! Try this: you go early to a new release movie because there are long lines and you want to get in quickly. Then you see a family walking down the sidewalk with a child in a wheelchair. They look at the long line, talk to each other and turn around to leave. What do you do? Offer them your place and move to the back of the line that looks like it's a mile long by now? Or, do you keep your mouth shut, figuring they'll just have to get here earlier next time like you did!

2. Hmm, are they your neighbors? Well, not really! You've never seen them on your block. But Jesus said... So, what do you do?

"The poor man probably would have died if a Samaritan hadn't come along and felt sorry for him. He saw the poor man lying there, suffering, and stopped to help. Even though the wounded man's people were not friendly to his "kind," the Samaritan knew he couldn't leave the man to die.

"He put disinfectant on the man's wounds and bandaged them. Then lifting the man onto his mule, the Samaritan took him to an inn and took care of him.

"The next day the Samaritan had to get back on the road so he gave the innkeeper some money and said, 'Please take care of this man until he is well. If you need more money, I'll pay you back on my way home.'

"Now," asked Jesus, "which of these three men was a neighbor to the one attacked by robbers?"

"The man who treated him kindly," answered the lawyer.

And Jesus said, "Go, and do the same."

Looking Good

John 11:1-54

Lazarus lived in the village of Bethany with his two sisters, Mary and Martha. Since their home was near Jerusalem, Jesus often stopped to visit them on his way to attend feasts at the temple. Jesus and his disciples were always welcome at the home of Mary, Martha and Lazarus. They loved Jesus a lot and believed in him. Their friendship was very special to Jesus.

One day while Jesus taught in the country east of the Jordan River, a messenger came from Bethany. Mary and Martha had sent the messenger to tell Jesus, "Lord, the one you love is sick." The anxious sisters thought Jesus would come right away and heal their brother. They knew he had great power, and they really needed him to use it—now!

But Jesus didn't go right away; instead, he explained to his disciples, "Lazarus' sickness is for the glory of God."

The sisters eagerly watched for Jesus and were really disappointed when the messenger returned without him! They watched their brother grow weaker and weaker. Then Lazarus died. They were grief-stricken. Why hadn't Jesus come?

They still hoped he would come; after all, he had raised the dead to life before. Night came but still Jesus didn't arrive. Finally, the neighbors and friends came to help get Lazarus' body ready for burial by wrapping it in strips of cloth. Then they carried his body to a cave where it was buried.

Mary and Martha followed, weeping bitterly. They saw their brother's body placed in the cave and watched the great stone rolled over the opening—still Jesus hadn't come.

Two days after receiving the message from Mary and Martha, Jesus said to his disciples, "Let's go back to Judea again."

The disciples didn't like the idea, and answered, "Master, when we were there before they tried to stone you. Why would you want to go back?" They didn't realize that Jesus had to finish the job God had sent him to do.

"Our friend Lazarus is asleep," Jesus told them. "I need to go and wake him up." At first the disciples thought Lazarus must have been getting better and was taking a long nap. Then Jesus told them, "Lazarus is dead. For your sakes I'm glad I wasn't there so you can have even more reason to believe."

Lazarus had been dead four days. The sisters thought sure it was too late for Jesus to help them now even if he did come. Friends came from Jerusalem to comfort the sisters but Jesus was the only one they wanted to see.

Finally, word came that Jesus and his disciples were close to the village. Martha ran to meet him. "Lord," she cried, "if only you'd been here, my brother wouldn't have died!"

To comfort her, Jesus said, "Your brother will rise again."

"I know he will be resurrected in the last day," she answered.

That's not what Jesus meant. He explained, "You don't have to wait for the last day. I am the resurrection and the life, right now. The one who believes in me will live, even though he or she dies. And those who live and believe in me will never die. Do you believe that?" he asked.

Martha answered, "Yes, Lord, I believe you are the Christ, the Son of God."

But Martha didn't really understand what Jesus meant. She went back inside to get her sister Mary. "The Master wants to talk to you, Mary," she said.

Mary ran to meet Jesus and found him sitting beside the road, resting. Falling at his feet she sobbed, "Lord, if you had been here my brother wouldn't have died!"

The Jews who had come from Jerusalem to comfort the sisters saw Mary leave the house in a hurry and thought she was going to Lazarus' grave, so they followed her. When they saw her fall, crying at Jesus' feet, they cried too.

"Where have you put Lazarus' body?" Jesus asked.

"Come see, Lord." They took him to the cave. Jesus wept in sympathy when he saw the sisters and their friends crying.

The friends whispered, "See how much he loved Lazarus!" Some others said *"Well, if he loved him so much, why didn't he do something to keep him from dying?* He opened blind eyes; couldn't he have healed Lazarus?"

While they talked Jesus walked up to the entrance of the cave. "Take away the stone," he said.

Martha exclaimed, "But Lord, he has been dead four days. By this time his body is decaying and stinks!"

Jesus answered, "Didn't I tell you that you would see the glory of God if you believed?"

POWER SURGE

1. Okay, so if Jesus loved Lazarus, Mary and Martha so much, why do you think He waited so long to go see them?
   a. He had more important things to finish where He was.
   b. He had brought people back to life before, but that was right after they died. It might take too long to get back to Lazarus. If He couldn't heal him, then Jesus would be embarrassed.
   c. If He waited four days it would show people the awesome power of God, and prepare them for His own death and resurrection.

2. How would you feel if you had been Mary or Martha?
   a. Really ticked that Jesus didn't come as soon as we called Him.
   b. Very sad that Jesus had let us down, especially after He'd stayed in our home so many times. We thought He was our friend!
   c. Everything will be okay as soon as Jesus gets here. He is the Son of God. We can trust Him.

3. So, how do you think Lazarus' body smelled after he'd been dead 4 days?
   a. Phew! Stinky!
   b. Not that bad! He was wrapped up and caves are usually cold, like refrigerators.
   c. I have no idea and I don't care to know!

The stone was rolled away. While the people watched, Jesus lifted his eyes to heaven and said, "Father, I thank you for listening to me. I know you always listen. I say this so the people who are here will believe you have sent me." Then Jesus looked into the door of the cave and shouted in a loud voice, "Lazarus, come out!"

Speechless, the people watched, their mouths dropping open. They could hardly believe their eyes—Lazarus, wrapped from head to toe in strips of linen, walked out of the cave! Jesus said, "Unwrap him and let him go." So Lazarus went home with his sisters and Jesus.

> **Reload**
> This was Jesus' last and most dramatic healing.

The Jews who had seen this miracle believed that Jesus was the Christ. Soon the Pharisees and chief priests heard what had happened at Bethany and called a meeting. "What are we going to do?" they asked. "If we let him go on, everyone will believe in him and the Romans will take away our nation."

From then on Jesus' enemies planned how they would capture and kill him.

Old School

Luke 14:7-24

After they had finished dinner at the Pharisee's house, Jesus began to teach. He had noticed that when the guests arrived, they each tried to get the best place. Jesus wanted them to think more of others than of themselves.

He said, "When you are invited to a wedding dinner, don't choose a place at the head table. If a more important person shows up you may be asked to give your seat to him, and then you'll be embarrassed; your face will turn red and you'll want to hide under the table. Instead, if you take the last place, your host can come and say 'Friend, come on up front and sit by me.' In other words, don't walk with your nose in the air because you'll probably fall flat on your face. Just be yourself."

Then Jesus turned to the host who had given the dinner and said, "When you have a dinner, don't invite your friends and relatives and rich neighbors who will return your invitation. Invite the poor, the crippled and the blind, the misfits and people

POWER SURGE

1. When you have a party who do you invite—the cool kids, just your closest friends—or do you include all kinds of kids?
2. In the lunchroom at school do you have a specific table that is just for "your group"? Or do you sit with different kids everyday? Do you invite others to sit with you?
3. Do you make excuses when you don't really want to go to someone's house? Are your excuses real or phony?

Reload

Think about this:

You make an excuse to God for not having your quiet time with Him—not reading the Bible, not praying (talking to Him).

He says to you, "You don't miss meals; you don't miss sleep; you have time for your favorite shows on TV. You have time for your friends when they call and want you to go to the mall. But you don't have time for ME? Truth is I'm just not important to you. I can handle that—can you?"

Hope your answer is "No, God, I need You! No more excuses!"

from the other side of the tracks. They can't repay you, but God will bless you beyond your wildest dreams."

One of the guests who heard Jesus' words said, "The person who gets to eat dinner in God's kingdom is really fortunate!"

All those sitting at the dinner table heard Jesus tell a story about the kingdom of God.

"A man was going to have a great dinner party and sent out a servant to invite a lot of guests. The guests were given the date and were asked to RSVP and put it on their calendars. They each said they would be happy to come to the party. The day of the dinner party came. Everything was ready—great decorations, fantastic food—the servant was sent out again to tell each guest, 'Come on; the food's on the table.' But they all made excuses for not coming."

"The first man said, 'I just bought some land outside of town and I need to go see it. Please excuse me this time.'"

"Another person said, 'I just bought five teams of oxen and I want to try them out. I'd like to be excused this time.'"

"A third said, 'I just got married, and I want to stay home with my wife. Won't you please excuse me?'"

"Everywhere the servant went the guests asked to be excused. The host was really upset when the servant came back without anyone to eat all the food. The host said to his servant, 'Go out in the streets and alleys to the poor, the homeless, the old—anyone who looks like they could use a square meal—bring them to dinner.'"

"The servant brought all the people he could find, but there was still room for more. The host said, 'Go into the country places and drag them in.' Finally the house was filled with hungry people who really enjoyed the good food."

Welcome Home!

Luke 15:11-32

Jesus told stories and this time there were sinners hanging around, listening to every word he said. He had already told stories about the lost sheep and the lost coin. Now came the story of the lost son—the son who chose to be lost.

"A man had two sons. One day the younger one said, 'Dad, would you please give me my share of the money that should come to me when you die? I want my money now. I have some plans and I need the money now.'"

"So the father split his property between his two sons. Before long the youngest son packed his bags and took off on a long trip. He spent his money like it was growing on trees; actually, he wasted most of it having a good time. At first, he had lots of friends who hung around enjoying his money with him. But when the money was gone, they were gone too."

POWER SURGE

1. Have you ever wished you were old enough and had your own money so you could leave home and live life the way you wanted to? No asking for permission to do stuff; no rules to live by, just freedom! Yeah, right! NOT!
2. Where did that kind of thinking get this young man? Was he really free?
3. Did the youngest son get all cleaned up before he came home? Or did he come home just the way he was?
4. Okay, now put yourself in the oldest son's place. How would you feel? Would you be happy your brother or sister was back home, or angry that people were making such a fuss over him or her?
5. Which of the two men was really lost?

"About this same time there was a famine in the country. People were out of jobs and hungry; soon the young man was hungry too. He finally got a job slopping (feeding) hogs for a farmer, but he still didn't have enough to eat. He even thought about eating some of the scraps he was throwing to the hogs."

"He was one miserable human being! Finally he came to his senses, 'Okay, this is really dumb! Dad's hired hands are treated better than this. They have plenty to eat, and here I am starving. I'm homesick! I'll go home to my dad and tell him I'm sorry; I was wrong. I don't deserve to be his son any longer, but I'd like to be one of his hired hands.' So he got up and started home."

"The father missed his younger son. He worried about him. Was he still alive? Was he dead? Was he okay? Every day he wished his son would come home. Every day he watched for him."

Reload

- The Prodigal Son chose to be lost. He thumbed his nose at God, at his father, at his family, and took off to live life his own way.

- Being FOUND doesn't' require cleaning up your act or changing your lifestyle. Think about this: fishermen clean the fish AFTER they're caught! So does Jesus.

- The youngest brother finally realized he was lost and headed for home. The oldest brother was lost but didn't even know it. He never ran away, never broke the rules, but missed the love his father wanted to give him because he was too stubborn and jealous. Hmm.

- Don't miss this: the father looked for his son everyday and was thrilled to have him home!

"One day the father saw someone coming in the distance. As the man got closer, the father could see he was dirty and ragged. Soon he recognized the man—it was his youngest son. He took off running down the lane, threw his arms around the young man and kissed him."

"Dad, the son said, 'I have sinned against heaven and against you. I don't deserve to be called your son. Would you please...?'"

"The father wasn't listening, but was calling the housekeeper, 'Hurry, bring some clean clothes and help him get dressed. Put a ring on his finger and shoes on his feet. Put some steaks on the grill, because we're having a party! Let's celebrate because my son has come home—the one I thought was lost has come home—he's found!' They had a great time."

"While all this was happening, the older son was out in the field working. When he finally came to the house and heard all the excitement, he asked, 'What's going on?'"

"The housekeeper said, 'Your brother has come home and your dad is having a party to celebrate because the boy is back, safe and sound.'"

"The older brother was not a happy camper! In fact, he was very angry—so angry he wouldn't join the party. When his father came out and tried to talk to him, he wouldn't listen. He just became angrier. He said, 'I stayed here, working for you all these years and never caused you any trouble, but did you ever throw a party for me and my friends? Now this son of yours comes back after throwing his money away on things you don't approve of, yet you celebrate him!'"

"The father knew his older son was jealous. He said, 'Son, try to understand, you stayed with me and everything I have is yours. I thought your brother was dead, but he's alive. We had to celebrate because he came home; he was lost, but now he's found.'"

Find the bolded words, below the word search, in the puzzle. Words can be found forwards and backwards—across and up and down.

```
B A E T F T I D E L C R I N T O H P Y W
W Y J N R E W O S E H T W E H K E D G O
I P I A T K S O C T M I S D X I W S T R
C R T V G P A P D H G F W E B J E L I N
K C O R E H T N O E S U O H O F D C A A
E A M E S T I O P N B Q E V K M D T S C
D E C S I K N G R W O T P R E O I N R I
H Y E L D Q H Y O B J S O W T R N E X L
U N J U S T J U D G E R I R A A G S E B
S E R F L I T G I A C F H M S R F O T U
B E W I C H M I G H O D A I L H E P I P
A R S C T E G S A K E S M B U H A R D E
N W M R Y B O O L P D G J I E D S O W H
D A I E C G L A S O S T N E L A T N E T
M S S M D E R K O D A V T F R E G J O D
E H O N F R E G N I L B U P K P L E I N
N L E U N I A F O L O S T C O I N S P A
Z O P Y S C G W I W T H U L D G E E T E
H E B R E H I S E S E O P Y H K E X P E
T D P E G F A J T T M J E R I H S N U S
O L I T N O B H A L S H O M S W A I D I
W G E K C O G R S P I E N T X I S R E R
H I J T E L E N I V R E S O S L E E B A
A N D I Y S U K E N A O F I N C O X P H
F S H G A T P O A M L R X H W I E G H P
```

GOOD SAMARITAN (Luke 10)
PRODIGAL SON (Luke 15)
PHARISEE AND THE PUBLICAN (Luke 18)
RICH FOOL (Luke 12)
TEN TALENTS (Matthew 25)
TWO DEBTORS (Luke 7)
UNJUST JUDGE (Luke 18)
UNMERCIFUL SERVANT (Matthew 18)
WEDDING FEAST (Luke 12)
WISE STEWARD (Luke 12)
HOUSE ON THE ROCK (Matthew 7, Luke 6)
LOST SHEEP (Matthew 18, Luke 15)
THE SOWER (Matthew 13, Mark 4, Luke 8)
THE TARES (Matthew 13)
LOST COIN (Luke 15)
WICKED HUSBANDMEN
   (Matthew 21, Mark 12, Luke 20)

See page 100 for answers

Reality Check

Luke 19:1-10

Jericho, the city whose walls had been brought down by Joshua and his trumpeters, was an important center for trade. In this city lived a very rich man named Zacchaeus, the head tax collector (not anyone's favorite person) for the region. When he heard Jesus was passing through Jericho on his way to Jerusalem, Zacchaeus was really excited. He'd heard lots of good things about this man and wanted to see who this Jesus was.

But Zacchaeus had a problem—he was too short to see over the heads of all the people who stood shoulder-to-shoulder in front of him. People were everywhere, crowded along the road, and most were a lot taller than Zacchaeus. He had to see Jesus! So he ran down the road until he found a tree with branches low enough for him to reach. He climbed into that sycamore tree and waited impatiently to see Jesus.

Soon travelers came down the road on their way to Jerusalem. The people of Jericho stood quietly—as if they were watching a parade—eager to catch a glimpse of Jesus. The travelers kept walking until they came to the sycamore tree, where Jesus and his disciples stopped for a few minutes. Though crowds of people lined both sides of the road, Jesus stopped, looked up and saw Zacchaeus.

"Zacchaeus," called Jesus, "hurry down here; I want to stop at your house and talk awhile." Zacchaeus couldn't believe it! He scrambled down that tree as quick as his short legs would take him—Jesus and the disciples were going home with him—he could hardly wait to talk to Jesus!

As Jesus and Zacchaeus headed for his house, some people who followed began to grumble and mutter, upset because Jesus was stopping in the home of a tax collector—a man they considered to be a horrible sinner. The Pharisees would not enter his house—they hated sinners.

Zacchaeus' heart was changed because Jesus wanted to be his friend and was willing to spend time with him. He told Jesus, "Lord, I'll give away half of my income to the poor, and if I have cheated anyone, I will pay back four times more than I took."

Jesus answered, "Today salvation has come to your house, for the Son of Man came to find and to save the lost."

We've been reading stories about friends Jesus met during his travels. You'll meet some more of His friends in the stories to come.

See how many of them you remember below. Match the person on the right to the phrase on the left.

1. Jesus had to look up in a tree to find _____.   Nicodemus

2. _____ baptized Jesus.   Judas

3. Jesus told _____ he had to be born again.   Thomas

4. _____ denied knowing Jesus three times.   Lazarus

5. Jesus was betrayed by _____.   disciples'

6. _____ doubted Jesus.   Simon

7. _____ was the mother of Jesus.   John

8. Jesus raised _____ from the dead.   Peter

9. Jesus was a carpenter like _____.   Zacchaeus

10. _____ was a tax collector, who followed Jesus.   Mary

11. Jesus visited Mary and _____, two sisters.   Joseph

12. Jesus washed the _____ feet.   Arimathea

13. Joseph of _____ loaned his tomb to Jesus.   Martha

14. _____ of Cyrene carried Jesus' cross.   Matthew

See page 100 for answers

POWER SURGE

1. Can you imagine how ridiculous it must have looked to see a grown man climb a tree just so he could see a parade of people coming down the street? What is it you've thought was important enough that you were willing to do something ridiculous? What is worth it?

2. Why do you suppose that of all the places Jesus could have stopped along the road, He chose to stop right beside the tree Zacchaeus had climbed?

3. Zacchaeus went to a lot of trouble to see Jesus, even to the point of looking ridiculous. Why do you suppose he was so eager to see Jesus?

4. How would you feel if Jesus walked up to you and said He wanted to go to your house for dinner? Would He be welcome in your home? What kind of meal would you have? What do you think you would talk about?

Farewell

Matthew 26:17-30; Mark 14:12-26 Luke 22:3-39; John 13

It was time to celebrate the Passover meal—Jesus knew his time on earth was coming to a close—this would be his last meal with the men he had come to love during the last three years they'd spent together. He also knew one of them had already made arrangements with the religious leaders to hand Jesus over to them, but not in front of a crowd because the people loved him. So, in order to outfox the traitor, Jesus kept plans for the meal a secret, except to a few that he trusted.

Jesus sent Peter and John on a secret mission with coded instructions: "Go to the city and look for a man carrying a pitcher of water; follow him (this was very unusual because men were never seen carrying water—that was woman's work). When he goes into a house, say to the owner, 'The Teacher asks, where is the guest room, where I may eat the Passover with my disciples?' "

POWER SURGE

1. Have you ever moved far away from your friends? Did they give you a going away/farewell party? What was it like? Did you laugh about things that had happened in the past? Were you sad?

2. Has anyone ever betrayed (deceived, let you down, was disloyal) you? How did you feel? What did you do about it? Were you able to forgive that person eventually?

3. What do you think about this story? How does it make you feel about Jesus? About Peter? About Judas?

The two went to the city and found things just as Jesus had said. The owner of the house led them to an upstairs room where Peter and John got everything ready for the meal.

When evening came Jesus and the other disciples joined Peter and John. It was a sad time for Jesus. This would be his farewell dinner with them, but they didn't know that yet. As they were eating Jesus told them this would be his last meal with them and that he was going to suffer.

They didn't understand; would Jesus really be taken away from them? Would men really try to kill him? Soon they were talking about other things at the table—who would be the greatest in Jesus' kingdom? They just didn't get it!

Reload
The twelve disciples were with Jesus night and day for three years and still, in the days before His death, they were guilty of jealousy, ambition, and denying Him.

Jesus knew what they were thinking. He wanted to teach them more about his true kingdom, about relationships, how important they were—so he decided to demonstrate rather than just talk. He got up from the table, took off his coat and tied a towel around his waist. Taking a basin of water, he began to wash their feet and dry them with the towel.

The disciples looked at each other, puzzled. Why was Jesus doing this? They had just washed their feet before coming into the upper room. Peter pulled his feet away from Jesus, embarrassed, and said, "Lord, you're not going to wash my feet!"

"If I don't wash your feet," said Jesus, "you can't be a part of what I'm doing."

Then Peter cried, "Lord, wash not only my feet, but also my hands and my head!"

Jesus answered, "Peter, you had a bath earlier so you don't need everything washed again, just your feet." Then Jesus put the towel away and put his coat back on.

He sat back down and asked, "Do you understand what I have done to you? You call me Lord, and Master, and that's okay because that is who I am. Now that I have washed your feet, you should wash one another's feet—I've set the example for you to follow. No servant is greater than his master; *an employee doesn't give orders to the employer*. If you know these things and live them, you will be blessed." Jesus was trying to teach them that to lead, one must serve.

After he finished talking to them Jesus became upset to the point the disciples could see it in his face. Then Jesus said, "One of you has betrayed me; one of you is a traitor."

The disciples looked around at each other, finding this really hard to believe. They all asked, "Lord, is it I?"

Jesus said, "I will give this piece of bread to the traitor after I've dipped it in the dish." Then, as everyone watched, Jesus gave the bread to Judas Iscariot and said, "Do what you have to do and get it over with quickly." Immediately Judas left the room and went out into the night.

The disciples didn't understand why Jesus said what he did to Judas, but because Judas took care of the money, they thought he was going to buy something for the feast or to give money to the poor.

After supper was over Jesus took bread, offered thanks, broke the bread and gave each disciple a piece. "Take this bread and eat it; it is a symbol of my body given for you; eat it and remember me." Then he took the cup, offered thanks, and passed it to them saying, "This cup is a new covenant (promise) in my blood poured out for you."

Jesus told them that he would soon die and leave them alone but that they shouldn't be afraid. When he told them he was leaving and they couldn't go with him now, but would follow him later, Peter said, "Lord, I want to go with you now! I'll never leave you!"

Jesus answered, "Peter, tonight before the rooster crows, you will deny three times that you ever knew me."

Then Jesus and his disciples sang a hymn as they left the upper room together, on their way to the Garden of Gethsemane.

Think about this: Jesus prayed this prayer for all of us, not just His disciples, after leaving the upper room.

Using a King James Version Bible, look up the scriptures listed after each sentence, fill in the blanks, then find the corresponding number on the puzzle and fill it in. (7D – the D stands for down. 13A – the A stands for across)

"This is life __7D__, that they might know thee the only true God, and __11A__ __17D__, whom thou hast sent." John 17:3

"I have glorified thee on the __4D__." John 17:4

"I have __19A__ thy name unto the men which thou gavest me out of the world." John 17:6

"I have given unto them the __10A__ which thou gavest me." John 17:8

"I __12A__ for them." John 17:9

"All mine are __5D__." John 17:10

"While I was with them in the __10D__, I kept them in thy __15A__: those that thou gavest me I have kept, and none of them is __6D__, but the son of __3A__." John 17:12

"These things I speak in the world, that they might have my __9D__ fulfilled in themselves." John 17:13

"I pray not that thou shouldest take them out of the world, but that thou shouldest keep them from the __20D__." John 17:15

"Sanctify them through thy __13A__." John 17:17

"For their sakes I __21A__ myself." John 17:19

"That they all may be __2D__; as thou, __1D__, art in me, and I in thee, that they also may be one in __18D__." John 17:21

"I in them, and thou in me, that they may be made __14D__ in one; and that the world may know that thou hast sent me, and hast __6A__ them, as thou hast loved me." John 17:23

"Thou lovedst me before the __8D__ of the world." John 17:24

"I have __16A__ unto them thy name." John 17:26

See page 100 for answers

Friendship Denied

Matthew 26:14-16; 36-75; Mark 14:10-11, 32-72; Luke 22:1-6, 39-71; John 18:1-27

Judas Iscariot went to the chief priests and asked, "What will you give me if I hand Jesus over to you?" They promised him thirty pieces of silver ($21.60 today). Judas knew about the Garden of Gethsemane because all of them had gone there often with Jesus.

After leaving the upper room, Jesus and the eleven disciples went to the garden. At the entrance, Jesus told eight of them, "Stay here while I go and pray." He took Peter, James and John, and went into the garden.

While he prayed the disciples fell asleep. They couldn't understand why he was so upset and had no idea how to comfort him. Jesus really wanted the three near, praying with him! Twice he woke up Peter, James and John, but they kept falling asleep. After the second time he said, "Peter, you fell asleep again? Can't you stay awake for even one hour?" Jesus went back to pray, and while he prayed in agony, alone, God sent an angel to comfort him and to give him strength.

Jesus knew he must die on the cross for the sins of the whole world so he could save all who wanted to live for him. Because he had a body and mind like ours, he really didn't want to suffer the pain his death would cause, and he didn't want to be left alone by those he loved. So he prayed, "Abba (Daddy), Father, you can take this away from me. But, please, not what I want—just what you want."

The third time Jesus woke up the sleeping disciples. "Come on, get up, let's go; the traitor's almost here." As he was speaking, they saw men carrying torches. Judas, the traitor, was with them. Stepping forward he said, "Rabbi!" and kissed Jesus on the cheek.

Jesus looked sadly at Judas and said, "Do you betray the Son of Man with a kiss?" Judas had told the men he would kiss Jesus so they would know which one they should take prisoner. Grabbing Jesus roughly, the soldiers led him away.

Peter drew a sword and struck one of the servants (Malchus), cutting off his ear. Jesus said to Peter, "Put up your sword." Then he touched the servant's ear and healed him. Peter hid in the shadows with the other frightened disciples.

The soldiers bound their prisoner and led him to the house of the high priest where Jesus' enemies waited. Peter followed way behind, not sure what he should do and really afraid the soldiers might take him prisoner too.

Peter stood in the courtyard, not far from where people had started a fire and were sitting around it trying to keep warm. A young girl looked his way several times and then said, "Aren't you one of his disciples?"

Peter was afraid and said, "No, I don't even know him." Peter got closer to the fire trying to get warm. Around the fire stood other men; one turned to Peter and said, "You are one of them." Again fear filled Peter's heart, and he replied, "No, I'm not! I don't know what you're talking about!"

A soldier standing by who had seen Peter use his sword said, "I saw you in the garden with him!" Peter cursed and said, "I don't know the man!" Just as Peter said those last words, the rooster crowed.

While all this had been happening with Peter, the high priests and others had been questioning Jesus and acting awful towards him. They led Jesus away; as he passed by, he looked sadly at Peter. Then Peter remembered Jesus' words, "Before the rooster crows, you will deny me three times." Peter turned blindly away from the fire, took off running and cried until he could hardly breathe.

POWER SURGE

True or False

1. Judas got big bucks for turning Jesus in to the soldiers. **T F**
2. Jesus took all 12 disciples with Him to pray in the garden. **T F**
3. Jesus took only Peter, James and John inside the garden with Him. **T F**
4. Peter, James and John kept falling asleep, instead of staying awake to keep Jesus company and to pray with him. **T F**
5. Jesus wasn't too worried about what was coming; after all, He was God's son. Nothing too awful could happen to Him. **T F**
6. Judas brought men with torches to arrest Jesus. **T F**
7. Judas walked up to Jesus and shook His hand; that was the signal. **T F**
8. When the soldiers grabbed Jesus, Peter lopped off the ear of one of them with a sword. **T F**
9. Jesus picked up the ear and reattached it to the man's head. **T F**
10. Peter never denied Jesus. **T F**

See page 100 for answers

No One is a Reject

Matthew 27:1-54; Mark 15:1-39; Luke 23:1-47; John 18:28-19:30

After Jesus' trial and his sentence of death, Judas became very upset and even sorry that he had betrayed Jesus. He never thought it would go this far! He only meant to force Jesus to free himself from his enemies by some miracle; but Jesus was allowing himself to be helpless in their hands.

Judas hurried back to the chief priests and scribes, saying, "I have sold an innocent man! I have sinned!" They looked at him with disgust and said, "We don't care! You have to answer for your sin." Judas tried to give back the 30 pieces of silver he had received for handing Jesus over to them, but they refused to take it back so Judas threw it on the floor of the temple and ran out. He was so hysterical he found a place away from everyone and hanged himself.

Soldiers took Jesus to the Roman governor, Pilate, who knew nothing about Jesus. Pilate took him into the courtroom and talked to him. When they came out he said, "This man is innocent." But the leaders made up more lies.

POWER SURGE

1. Who is Jesus?
2. Who was responsible for Jesus' death?
3. Could God or Jesus have stopped this whole process?
4. Why did Jesus have to die?
5. What did you learn from Judas?

Pilate finally said, "This man is Galilean; let Herod decide his fate." Herod was a son of the king who had tried to kill Jesus when he was a baby—the one who had John the Baptist beheaded.

When the soldiers brought Jesus, bound with chains, to Herod he was glad. He hoped Jesus would do some miracles, but Jesus wouldn't answer even one of Herod's questions. Along with his soldiers, Herod mocked Jesus, dressing him in rich robes, and pretending to honor him as a king. Then he sent Jesus back to Pilate.

Now Pilate's wife was terrified about this whole thing with Jesus; that night she had even dreamt about him. She pleaded with her husband to set Jesus free, saying, "He is a good man, not guilty, and shouldn't be put to death."

Pilate wanted to set Jesus free too, and told the mob, "Both Herod and I have examined this man and found him not guilty."

But the mob wanted blood so Pilate tried to appease them. He sentenced Jesus to a beating, even though it was illegal to beat (scourge) an innocent man. They used leather straps with fragments of bones and steel tied on the ends so that when the prisoners were beaten, their skin was torn off their bodies. Many died from the beating and were never crucified. Most screamed from the pain and eventually lost consciousness. Jesus did none of these—he remained conscious the whole time, never cried out or screamed.

After the beating, Jesus was brought back to Pilate who thought sure Jesus could now be released. But still the mob wanted him dead! It was the custom at the time of Passover to release one condemned prisoner. Barabbas was a murderer, a terrorist, a thief—a wicked man who had caused a lot of problems for everyone, including the Sanhedrin. Pilate asked, "Should I release to you Barabbas, the wicked man, or Jesus?"

With loud, angry cries the mob shouted "Set Barabbas free!"

Pilate asked, "What should I do with Jesus?" and they shouted, "Crucify him! Crucify him!"

Taking a basin of water, Pilate washed his hands and said, "I will not accept responsibility for Jesus' death. He is innocent!"

The mob shouted, "We will bear the blame. Let his blood be on our heads!"

The trial was over—Pilate released Jesus to the Roman soldiers for crucifixion.

The soldiers put a crown of thorns on Jesus' head. They put a reed in his hand and bowed before him, saying, "Hail, King of the Jews!" They blindfolded him, spit on him, and hit him, saying, "If you are the Son of God tell us who struck you!" Jesus didn't say a word. Finally, the soldiers took off the purple robe, dressed him in his own clothes and led him away to be crucified. They made Jesus and the two thieves carry heavy crosses to their own crucifixion.

A crowd of curious people followed Jesus, the thieves, and the soldiers to the place of crucifixion. Many in the crowd were Jesus' enemies, who took the opportunity to strike at him with whips and sticks; others were friends who longed to help but could not. During this excruciating journey, Jesus kept his composure, even speaking to women along the way who were crying. He was so weary from being up all night and from the beatings, he fell several times beneath the weight of the heavy cross. Finally, soldiers called a stranger from the crowd to help carry it.

Reload

- Darkness is a sign of God's judgment
- During the 3 hours that darkness covered the earth, the sin of all people penetrated Jesus' soul until He became sin itself
- God's nature demands justice—He turned His back on Jesus during the darkness. At the end of that 3-hour timeframe Jesus cried out, "My God, My God, why have you abandoned me?"
- What we learn from Judas
  - We can act spiritual—like a disciple—but not really be committed and dedicated to God
  - We can always rationalize bad behavior
  - We can spend time with God's people but that doesn't make us a Christian—only living for God, listening to Him and making right choices, allows us to wear that label—Christian
- Jesus says to us:
  - *There is nothing you can do, no matter how bad, that will make me stop loving you!*
  - *There is nothing you can do, no matter how good, that will make me love you any more!*

On the hillside of Calvary the crowd stopped. Soldiers removed the prisoners' clothing and drove nails through their hands and feet into the crosses. Then they raised the crosses high in the air and pounded them firmly in the ground, leaving the prisoners to hang there until they died. Jesus hung on the cross for 6 hours, from 9 A.M. until 3 P.M. in the afternoon.

As soon as the cross was placed in the ground Jesus prayed, "Father, forgive them, they don't know what they're doing."

A sign hung above Jesus' head with the words, "This is Jesus, the King of the Jews," written in the three main languages of that day—Latin, Greek and Hebrew.

One of the thieves who was crucified with Jesus made fun of him and insulted him: "Aren't you the Christ? Save yourself and us!" The other thief said to the first, "We deserve to die, but this man hasn't done anything wrong." To Jesus he said, "Lord, remember me when you enter your kingdom."

Jesus answered him, *"Don't worry, today you will join me in paradise."*

Jesus' friends stood at the foot of his cross in shock, crying and praying. Among them were his mother, Mary, and John, one of his disciples. Jesus said to John, "This is now your mother, take care of her." And to Mary he said, "This (John) is now your son."

Jesus' enemies also stood around the cross insulting him with statements such as, "If you are the King of the Jews, why don't you come down off that cross and save yourself?"

Around noon the sky suddenly grew very dark, the sun stopped shining—a total blackout—for three hours. The curtain at the temple tore right down the middle, from top to bottom. Then Jesus cried with a loud voice, "It is finished!"

The Roman captain standing near the cross, turned to his soldiers and said, "This was a good man!"

The words in bold in each scripture below can be found in the word search. Circle each word as you find it.

```
S B O N H O M E L C K I S D J
D G V M E D Y F P T I V R I F
N E K A S R O F O R E B I S N
E A N I C E T H A R T E L C A
M V O F R H A S I O G M Y I Q
M A W S I E P L Y W T I D P S
O S E R H O Y T Z I N U V L E
C A S L E V M E R U I K A E P
H T E T B O F I S O N R C I S
O B P R U I P O V I G E S O T
M I E E G S R W H E D O B F U
O D F H I X K A R O L A I P M
J E C T O R I E V F E N R T J
E L A O V L H N I K I P T A V
T I Z M I T D E G S S D O L P
V F Q U A W M I H E T E W R F
K S A F B E W E O N A M O W I
O C I T H S D N A H E T H E M
```

"**Father, forgive them;** for they **know** not what they do." —Luke 23:34

"**Verily** I say unto thee, Today shalt thou be with me in **paradise**." —Luke 23:43

"He saith unto his **mother, Woman, behold** thy **son**! Then saith he to the **disciple**, Behold thy mother." —John 19:26-27

"My God, my God, why hast thou **forsaken** me?" —Matthew 27:46

"I **thirst**." —John 19:28

"It is **finished**." —John 19:30

"Father, into thy **hands** I **commend** my **spirit**." —Luke 23:46

See page 100 for answers

Ready or Not!

Matthew 28:1-15; Mark 16:1-11; Luke 24:1-12; John 20:1-18

The hours dragged slowly for the Roman soldiers who guarded Jesus' grave. No one had tried anything, no one had come by—his followers were probably laughing at the religious leaders for being afraid.

As dawn came the ground began to tremble—another earthquake had come. The scared soldiers saw a large angel come down from the sky, roll the stone away from the tomb where they had put Jesus' body, and then sit on it. The angel's face was like lightning and his garments were as white as snow. The soldiers fell to the ground, trembling and helpless, as if they were dead. As soon as they were able to move, they got up and ran to the city to report to Jesus' enemies.

When the women came to prepare Jesus' body for burial, they saw the stone rolled away; when they walked inside, the tomb was empty. They looked all over inside but could not find the body of their Lord. Mary Magdalene ran to tell Peter and John that Jesus' body had disappeared.

After Mary left, the other women saw an angel in the tomb—it scared them so, they fell on their knees and put their faces to the ground.

The angel said, "Don't be afraid. Why are you looking for the living in a cemetery? Jesus is not here; he has risen as he said. Run and tell his disciples that he is alive and will meet them in Galilee."

The women ran from the place, excited yet trembling with fear. It just seemed too wonderful to be true. Still, they believed and hurried to tell the disciples and other friends that Jesus was alive!

The disciples couldn't believe it—Peter and John ran to see for themselves. When they got to the tomb, they didn't find anyone—it was empty—but they saw the clothes that Joseph had wrapped around Jesus' body.

POWER SURGE

1. The disciples and many others who had followed Jesus for three years were astonished that He was gone from the tomb. He had told them over and over that He would die, but would live again. They had seen the miracles He had performed—the last one, raising Lazarus from the dead. Why do you think they were so surprised? Would you have been surprised?

2. How do you think the chief priests and religious leaders reacted to the earthquake that tore the curtain in two, and then to the news that Jesus' body was gone? Do you think they were afraid? Sorry for what they'd had done to Jesus?

3. What would it take to convince you that Jesus was alive, if you had seen Him die on the cross?

Peter and John returned to their homes, convinced that Jesus was alive once more.

Mary Magdalene hadn't stayed in the garden long enough to hear the angel's message. Now she returned, longing to find where Jesus had been taken. She stood by the empty tomb and wept. Stooping down and looking at the grave she saw two angels—one sitting at the head and the other at the foot—where Jesus' body had been.

They asked her, "Woman, why are you crying?"

She replied, "Because they have taken away my Lord and I have no idea where they put him." Then turning around she saw Jesus standing there, but tears blinded her eyes and she didn't recognize him.

He too asked, "Why are you crying?"

Thinking he was the gardener, she said, "Sir, if you carried him away, tell me where you put him so I can go care for his body."

Jesus said, "Mary!" She turned to face him and said, "Teacher!" She was so happy! Jesus said, "Go tell my brothers that I am returning to my Father and your Father, to my God and your God."

While these things were happening, the soldiers were telling the chief priests what had taken place in the garden. Shaken by the news, they quickly called Jesus' other enemies—all anxious about what would happen now. Jesus' enemies offered the soldiers a large sum of money if they would promise not to tell anyone that Jesus had risen, or that an angel had opened the tomb.

The soldiers didn't care about these people or their religion so they were happy to take the money. When they were later questioned about the disappearance of Jesus' body, they said the disciples stole it while they slept.

Words below the cross are ones connected with Christ's death and resurrection. Find them in the word search and circle them.

```
              N E D R A G
              I P A M O C
              B S D L E R
              A E G C T O
              T O I L A S
    J U D A S T E D E L S K O M R F
    E C P E H O G A G I E I B I I T
    B A R A B B A S N P N S E J S E
    O R I D A S E N A M E S H T E G
    A C R U C I F Y R V V A C O N H
              J E T E O I
              A B I S S G
              I H S U I R
              T E T R L O
              A S O R V F
              H E M E E N
              C I B C R E
              A O S T I G
              R K V I H E
              A N W O R C
              S T O N E F
```

ANGEL	GARDEN	RISEN
ARRESTED	GETHSEMANE	ROBE
BARABBAS	GOLGOTHA	SILVER
CROSS	JUDAS	STONE
CROWN	KISS	THIEVES
CRUCIFY	PILATE	TOMB
FORGIVENESS	RESURRECTION	TREE

See page 100 for answers

I Doubt It!

Luke 24:36-48; John 20:19-31

The disciples were hiding in a room behind bolted doors, expecting Jesus' enemies to show up at any minute to take them all away and kill them. All of a sudden Jesus appeared in the room—not through the door or a window—he just appeared.

"Peace be with you," he said.

But the disciples didn't feel any peace! Was this a ghost? They were *scared half to death!*

Jesus knew what they were thinking and said, "Why are you so afraid? Why do you doubt what you see? I'm not a ghost. Look at my hands and my feet. I'm here—in the flesh. Touch me and you'll know that I'm not a ghost—a ghost doesn't have flesh and bones."

The disciples looked at his hands and feet—the scars were there. It really was the Lord! They were so amazed they didn't know what to do.

"Do you have anything here to eat?" Jesus asked. They gave him broiled fish and Jesus ate it in front of them, another sign that he really was alive.

Then Jesus tried once again to help them understand the Scriptures. He said, "Christ had to suffer and to rise from the dead on the third day. Now repentance and forgiveness of sins will be preached in his name to everyone—starting now. And you are the first to hear it and see it—you are witnesses."

The disciples were so excited about their visit with Jesus! Thomas hadn't been with them when Jesus came but they made sure to tell him, "We have seen the Lord."

But Thomas wouldn't take their word for it, "Unless I see and touch the scars in his hands and feel his side, I won't believe he's alive."

Eight days later the disciples were together again in a room with the doors shut—this time Thomas was with them. Just as before, suddenly Jesus stood in the room with them and said, "Peace to you!"

POWER SURGE

1. When Jesus just appeared through a locked door the disciples were scared silly. How do you think you'd react if someone just appeared in your room? Pass out? Faint? Run?

2. Have you ever been so frightened you wanted to hide? What happened that caused you to feel that way?

3. Do you believe easily? Or, are you like Thomas and need proof?

4. The disciples made sure Thomas rejoined them at meetings. Do you have friends like Thomas who need you to help "bring" them to the Lord?

While the disciples once again marveled at the way the Lord just appeared, Jesus spoke directly to Thomas, "Put your fingers in my hands and place your hand in my side. Don't doubt; believe."

Falling to his knees Thomas said, "My Lord and my God!"

Jesus told Thomas, "You believe because you have seen me. *Even better blessings are in store for those who believe without seeing.*"

Reload

- After Jesus appeared to the disciples they changed dramatically
- After the crucifixion they were broken, defeated, scared, guilt-ridden
- After Jesus rose and reappeared to them, they were bold, unafraid, motivated

Xtra Stuff

Maps

Answers

Discovering the Bible

Read the Bible in a Year

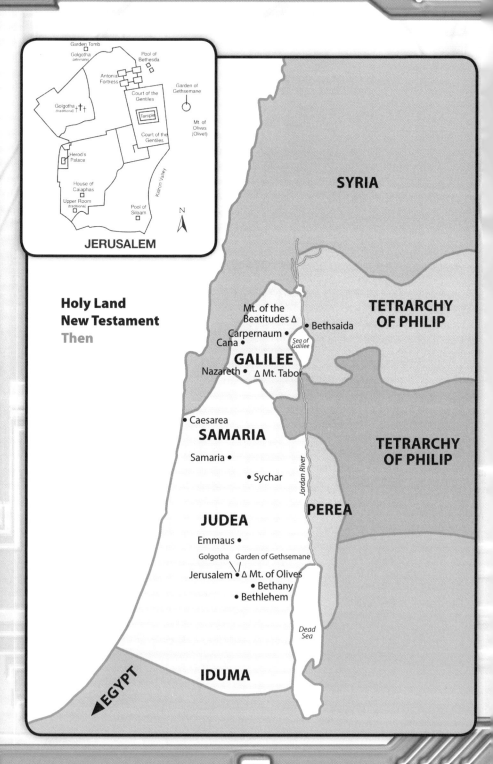

Answers

Discovering the Bible (pg 101)
1. 39, 2. 27, 3. Genesis, Malachi, 4. Psalms, (150), 5. Genesis, Exodus, Leviticus, Numbers, Deuteronomy, 6. Adam, Eve, 7. Genesis 6—9, 8. 90, (Genesis 17:17), 9. Exodus 20, 10. Job, (19:25), 11. Shadrach, Meshach, and Abenego, (Daniel 3), 12. Matthew, Revelation, 13. Tie of 3 books, 2 & 3 John, Jude, 14. John

He's Here! (pg 22)
True or False or Who Knows?

1. W (not! — no one really knows)
2. F (it could have been a cave; all we know for sure was that it was a manger)
3. W (could have been, but some say it was Michael)
4. W (all we know is that a donkey was with them)
5. F (nope — a feeding trough for animals)
6. F (nope — see Luke 2:12)
7. F (not! — see Surge Protector!)
8. T (somewhere in Israel)
9. T (all babies cry sometime!)
10. F (see Luke 2:1, 4)

Safe at Home (pg 26)
Jesus grew in wisdom and stature, and in favor with God and men. Luke 2:52

Make Some Noise (pg 33)
1. T, 2. F, 3. F, 4. F, 5. T, 6. F, 7. F, 8. T

Reborn (pg 35)
God didn't go to all the trouble of sending his Son merely to point an accusing finger, telling the world how bad it was. He came to help, to put the world right again.

Work & Pray (pg 41)
Our father which art in heaven, hallowed be thy name. Thy kingdom come. Thy will be done in earth, as it is in heaven. Give us this day our daily bread. And forgive us our debts, as we forgive our debtors. And lead us not into temptation, but deliver us from evil: For thine is the kingdom, and the power, and the glory, for ever. Amen.

```
P A S C E T Y M O L W R B O T K M E
L A R Z A H G E F H I J E H L O F I
E J O D G I V E N O E V G E D T O W
D Y T X E N M A K I C A S I M A R H
O A B L R E M E S B I E V P Y Y G A
E R E S G I P O J Q U H T E R E I N
B O D A H L V E D I F E M A N I V T
J S E M S D O L A G W L X T G I E Y
O F I D A E L R A C N E V I L M O S
L A R I T W E K Y P T I S E P T L D
H E L A D O C V I E G E K T I R E O
E Y I M E L S Z A M E N A V E N W A
A T D O K L E R P W D T I H A R I F
G I V A C A T E F S I E T G Y E L A
E O B R E H N I D O J A V L B A L K
A P O W E R T E N E F I C T O S G E
F I Q U O A B G A R E V I L E D V E
S T E H S U T E K E P V N O M I A J
```

This is Boring (pg 42)
True of False

1. T, 2. T, 3. F, 4. T, 5. T, 6. T

```
S P R A F B M E L G I K H A D
T H A D D E A U S J W C O J S
I O M U O F T M Q A O E N L I
B H I J R P T A N M I H E B T
L T P R S G H O W E R D N A O
O E C E A R E N F S T A J R D
D I L T O C W O E M I D E T P
E K U E T J S A B S E T C H E
M A H P S E T I N G A J I O F
S G W N A H E N S U R L E L M
N Y T O O S O L D A I B H O J
A F Y M Z M R I E P D Q E M C
W J A I I C E J G T W U N E S
E S E S B S L A D U F E J W R
L K P X E H M O K E J A M E S
```

Truth & Consequences
(pg 44)

You are the <u>salt</u> of the <u>earth</u>. But if the salt loses its saltiness, how can it be made <u>salty</u> again? It is no longer <u>good</u> for anything, except to be <u>thrown</u> out and <u>trampled</u> by men. You are the <u>light</u> of the <u>world</u>. A <u>city</u> on a hill <u>cannot</u> be <u>hidden</u>. Neither do <u>people</u> light a <u>lamp</u> and put it <u>under</u> a <u>bowl</u>. Instead they <u>put</u> it on a <u>stand</u>, and it <u>gives</u> light to everyone in the <u>house</u>. In the same way, let your light <u>shine</u> before men, that they may <u>see</u> your <u>good</u> <u>deeds</u> and <u>praise</u> your <u>Father</u> in <u>heaven</u>

Don't Worry; Be Happy *(pg 46)*
The disciple woke him and said to him, "Teacher, don't you care if we drown?" He got up, rebuked the wind and said to the waves, "Quiet! Be still!" Then the wind died down and it was completely calm.

Trust Factor
(pg 50, 51)

began, multitude, country, victuals, meat, fifties, heaven, before, fragments, twelve, baskets, lodge, five, thousand, company, brake, filled

f	g	j	y	r	t	n	u	o	c	s
k	r	b	e	g	a	n	q	a	v	e
f	b	a	s	k	e	t	s	g	e	i
i	r	j	g	w	m	y	h	p	d	t
l	a	c	o	m	p	a	n	y	u	f
l	k	d	t	w	e	l	v	e	t	i
e	e	g	d	o	l	n	e	v	i	f
d	n	a	s	u	o	h	t	p	t	t
b	v	i	c	t	u	a	l	s	l	y
x	o	c	n	e	v	a	e	h	u	k
z	l	w	b	e	f	o	r	e	m	b

Bright Lights & Strange Visitors
(pg 55, 56)
1. F, 2. F, 3. F, 4. T, 5. T

Call 911 *(pg 58)*
Miracles of Jesus, Calmed the storm, Walked on water, Fish and loaves, Water and wine, Two blind men, Crippled women, Large catch of fish

Play to Win *(pg 60)*
1. F, 2. F, 3. T,

70x7 *(pg 62)*
FORGIVE

Body Language
(pg 69)

Welcome Home (pg 77)

```
B A E T F T I D E L C R I N T O H P Y W
W Y J N R E W O S E H T W E H K E D G O
I P I A T K S O C T M I S D X I W S T R
C R T V G P A P D H G F W E B J E L I N
K C O R E H T N O E S U O H O F D C A A
E A M E S T I O P N B Q E V K M D T S C
D E C S I K N G R W O T P R E O I N R I
H Y E L D Q H Y O B J S O W T R N E X L
U N J U S T J U D G E R I R A A G S E B
S E R F L I T G I A C F H M S R F O T U
B E W I C H M I G H O D A I L H E P I P
A R S C T E G S A K E S M B U H A R D E
N W M R Y B O O L P D G J I E D S O W H
D A I E C G L A S O S T N E L A T N E T
M S S M D E R K O D A V T F R E G J O D
E H O N F R E G N I L B U P K P L E I N
N L E U N I A F O L O S T C O I N S P A
Z O P Y S C G W I W T H U L D G E E T E
H E B R E H I S E S E O P Y H K E X P E
```

Reality Check (pg 79)

1. Zacchaeus, 2. John, 3. Nicodemus, 4. Peter,
5. Judas, 6. Thomas, 7. Mary, 8. Lazarus,
9. Joseph, 10. Matthew, 11. Martha,
12. disciples', 13. Aramathea, 14. Simon

Farewell (pg 83)

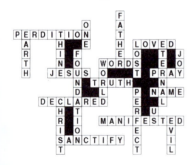

Friendship Denied (pg 85)

1. **F**, 2. **F**, 3. **T**, 4. **T**, 5. **F**,
6. **T**, 7. **F**, 8. **T**, 9. **T**, 10. **F**

Jesus Was a Reject (pg 89)

```
S B O N H O M E L C K I S D J
D G V M E D Y F P T I V R I F
N E K A S R O F O R E B I S N
E A N I C E T H A R T E L C A
M V O F R H A S I O G M Y I Q
M A W S I E P L Y W T I D P S
O S E R H O Y T Z I N U V L E
C A S L E V M E R U I K A E P
H T E T B O F I S O N R C I S
O B P R U I P O V I G E S O T
M I E E G S R W H E D O B F U
O D F H I X K A R O L A I P M
J E C T O R I E V F E N R T J
E L A O V L H N I K I P T A V
T I Z M I T D E G S S D O L P
V F Q U A W M I H E T E W R F
K S A F B E W E O N A M O W I
O C I T H S D N A H E T H E M
```

Ready or Not (pg 92)

```
            N E D R A G
            I P A M O C
            B S D L E R
            A E G C T O
            T O I L A S
J U D A S T E D E L S K O M R F
E C P E H O G A G I E I B I I T
B A R A B B A S N P N S E J S E
O R I D A S E N A M E S H T E G
A C R U C I F Y R V V A C O N H
            J E T E O I
            A B I S S G
            I H S U I R
            T E T R L O
            A S O R V F
            H E M E E N
            C I B C R E
            A O S T I G
            R K V I H E
            A N W O R C
            S T O N E F
```

Discovering the Bible

As you're reading through the Bible in a year, or whenever you know the answers, fill in the blanks below. Challenge: make a copy of this page; fill in what you know now. After you've finished reading, go back and answer the questions again—in the book this time—and see how much you have learned!

1. How many books are in the Old Testament?
2. How many books are in the New Testament?
3. What are the first and last books in the Old Testament?
4. What book in the Old Testament has the most chapters?
5. What are the first five books of the Bible/Old Testament?
6. Who were the first man and woman?
7. Where is the story of Noah found?
8. How old was Sarah when God told her she would have a child?
9. In what book of the Bible do we find the 10 Commandments?
10. Who said, "I know that my Redeemer lives"?
11. What three men were thrown into a fiery furnace?
12. What are the first and last books in the New Testament?
13. What book of the New Testament has the shortest chapter?
14. Who wrote the Book of Revelation?

See page 98 for answers

What part of the Bible did you like the best? Why?

_____

_____

_____

What is your biggest question about the Bible?

_____

_____

_____

Miracles of Jesus

Jesus healed people, used supernatural power on nature, and brought dead people back to life.

Man with leprosy cleansed — Matthew 8:2-3
A servant is healed — Matthew 8:5-13
Peter's mother-in-law cured — Matthew 8:14-15
Calmed the storm — Matthew 8:23-27
Two men from Gadara are healed — Matthew 8:28-32
Paralyzed man healed — Matthew 9:2-7
Jairus' daughter raised from the dead — Matthew 9:18-25
Woman with bleeding is healed — Matthew 9:20-22
Two blind men see — Matthew 9:27-31
Deaf, demon-possessed man is healed — Matthew 9:32-33
Man with withered hand is healed — Matthew 12:9-13
Blind, mute man can see & talk — Matthew 12:22
5,000 + are fed — Matthew 14:16-21
Jesus walks on water — Matthew 14:25
Gentile woman's daughter healed — Matthew 15:22-28
4,000 are fed — Matthew 15:32-38
Epileptic boy is cured — Matthew 17:14-18
Coin found in fish's mouth — Matthew 17:24-27
Two blind men can see — Matthew 20:30-34
Fig tree withered — Matthew 21:18-19
Unclean spirit is cast out — Mark 1:23
Deaf mute can hear & talk — Mark 7:31-35
Blind man at Bethsaida healed — Mark 8:22-25
Large catch of fish — Luke 5:4-7
Widow's son raised from the dead — Luke 7:11-15
Woman with bent back is cured — Luke 13:11-13
Man with dropsy is healed — Luke 14:1-4
Ten lepers cleansed — Luke 17:11-19
Servant's ear reattached — Luke 22:51
Water turned to wine — John 2:1-10
A son is healed — John 4:46-53
Crippled man healed in pool — John 5:1-9
Man born blind can see — John 9:1-12
Lazarus raised from dead — John 11:38-44
Another larger catch of fish — John 21:4-6

The Stories (Parables) Jesus Told

The Candle Under a Bush – Matthew 5:14-16

The House on Rock & Sand – Matthew 7:24-27

The Sower – Matthew 13:3-23

The Weeds – Matthew 13:24-30

The Mustard Seed – Matthew 13:31-32

The Hidden Treasure – Matthew 13:44

The Pearl – Matthew 13:45-46

The Net – Matthew 13:47-50

The Lost Sheep – Matthew 18:12-14

The Unmerciful Servant – Matthew 18:23-35

The Workers in the Vineyard – Matthew 20:1-16

Two Sons – Matthew 21:28-32

The Tenants – Matthew 21:33-44

The Wedding Banquet – Matthew 22:2-14

Ten Virgins – Matthew 25:1-13

The Talents – Matthew 25:14-30

The Growing Seed – Mark 4:26-29

The Good Samaritan – Luke 10:30-37

The Rich Fool – Luke 12:16-21

The Yeast – Luke 13:20-21

The Great Banquet – Luke 14:16-24

The Lost Coin – Luke 15:8-10

The Prodigal Son – Luke 15:11-32

The Shrewd Manager – Luke 16:1-13

The Rich Man & Lazarus – Luke 16:19-31

The Persistent Widow – Luke 18:1-8

The Pharisee & the Tax Collector – Luke 18:9-14

The Ten Minas – Luke 19:11-27

Read the Bible in a Year

January

1
- Genesis 1—3
- Matthew 1

2
- Genesis 4—6
- Matthew 2

3
- Genesis 7—9
- Matthew 3

4
- Genesis 10—12
- Matthew 4

5
- Genesis 13—15
- Matthew 5:1-26

6
- Genesis 16—17
- Matthew 5:27-48

7
- Genesis 18—19
- Matthew 6:1–18

8
- Genesis 20—22
- Matthew 6:19–34

9
- Genesis 23—24
- Matthew 7

10
- Genesis 25—26
- Matthew 8:1–17

11
- Genesis 27—28
- Matthew 8:18–34

12
- Genesis 29—30
- Matthew 9:1–17

13
- Genesis 31—32
- Matthew 9:18–38

14
- Genesis 33—35
- Matthew 10:1-20

15
- Genesis 36—38
- Matthew 10:21-42

16
- Genesis 39—40
- Matthew 11

17
- Genesis 41—42
- Matthew 12:1-23

18
- Genesis 43—45
- Matthew 12:24–50

19
- Genesis 46—48
- Matthew 13:1-30

20
- Genesis 49—50
- Matthew 13:31-58

21
- Exodus 1—3
- Matthew 14:14-21

22
- Exodus 4—6
- Matthew 14:22-36

23
- Exodus 7—8
- Matthew 15:1-20

24
- Exodus 9—11
- Matthew 15:21-39

25
- Exodus 12—13
- Matthew 16

26
- Exodus 14—15
- Matthew 17

27
- Exodus 16—18
- Matthew 18:1-20

28
- Exodus 19—20
- Matthew 18:21-35

29
- Exodus 21—22
- Matthew 19

30
- Exodus 23—24
- Matthew 20:1-16

31
- Exodus 25—26
- Matthew 20:17-34

February

1. ☐ Exodus 27—2
   ☐ Matthew 21:1-22

2. ☐ Exodus 29—30
   ☐ Matthew 21:23-46

3. ☐ Exodus 31—33
   ☐ Matthew 22:1-22

4. ☐ Exodus 34—35
   ☐ Matthew 22:23-46

5. ☐ Exodus 36—38
   ☐ Matthew 23:1-22

6. ☐ Exodus 39—40
   ☐ Matthew 23:23-39

7. ☐ Leviticus 1—3
   ☐ Matthew 24:1-28

8. ☐ Leviticus 4—5
   ☐ Matthew 24:29-51

9. ☐ Leviticus 6—7
   ☐ Matthew 25:1-30

10. ☐ Leviticus 8—10
    ☐ Matthew 25:31-46

11. ☐ Leviticus 11—12
    ☐ Matthew 26:1-25

12. ☐ Leviticus 13
    ☐ Matthew 26:26-50

13. ☐ Leviticus 14
    ☐ Matthew 26:51-75

14. ☐ Leviticus 15—16
    ☐ Matthew 27:1-26

15. ☐ Leviticus 17—18
    ☐ Matthew 27:27-50

16. ☐ Leviticus 19—20
    ☐ Matthew 27:51-66

17. ☐ Leviticus 21—22
    ☐ Matthew 28

18. ☐ Leviticus 23—24
    ☐ Mark 1:1-22

19. ☐ Leviticus 25
    ☐ Mark 1:23-45

20. ☐ Leviticus 26—27
    ☐ Mark 2

21. ☐ Numbers 1—2
    ☐ Mark 3:1-19

22. ☐ Numbers 3—4
    ☐ Mark 3:20-35

23. ☐ Numbers 5—6
    ☐ Mark 4:1-20

24. ☐ Numbers 7—8
    ☐ Mark 4:21-41

25. ☐ Numbers 9—11
    ☐ Mark 5:1-20

26. ☐ Numbers 12—14
    ☐ Mark 5:21-43

27. ☐ Numbers 15—16
    ☐ Mark 6:1-29

28. ☐ Numbers 17—21
    ☐ Mark 6:30-56

March

1. ☐ Numbers 22—25
   ☐ Mark 7

2. ☐ Numbers 26—27
   ☐ Mark 8:1-21

3. ☐ Numbers 28—30
   ☐ Mark 8:22-38

4. ☐ Numbers 31—33
   ☐ Mark 9:1-29

5. ☐ Numbers 34—36
   ☐ Mark 9:30-50

6. ☐ Deuteronomy 1—2
   ☐ Mark 10:1-31

7. ☐ Deuteronomy 3—4
   ☐ Mark 10:32-52

8. ☐ Deuteronomy 5—7
   ☐ Mark 11:1-18

9. ☐ Deuteronomy 8—10
   ☐ Mark 11:19-33

10. ☐ Deuteronomy 11—13
    ☐ Mark 12:1-27

11. ☐ Deuteronomy 14—16
    ☐ Mark 12:28-44

12. ☐ Deuteronomy 17—19
    ☐ Mark 13:1-20

13. ☐ Deuteronomy 20—22
    ☐ Mark 13:21-37

14. ☐ Deuteronomy 23—25
    ☐ Mark 14:1-26

15. ☐ Deuteronomy 26—27
    ☐ Mark 14:27-53

16. ☐ Deuteronomy 28—29
    ☐ Mark 14:54-72

17. ☐ Deuteronomy 30—31
    ☐ Mark 15:1-25

18. ☐ Deuteronomy 32—34
    ☐ Mark 15:26-47

19. ☐ Joshua 1—3
    ☐ Mark 16

20. ☐ Joshua 4—6
    ☐ Luke 1:1-20

21. ☐ Joshua 7—9
    ☐ Luke 1:21-38

22. ☐ Joshua 10—12
    ☐ Luke 1:39-56

23. ☐ Joshua 13—15
    ☐ Luke 1:57-80

24. ☐ Joshua 16—18
    ☐ Luke 2:1-24

25. ☐ Joshua 19—21
    ☐ Luke 2:25-52

26. ☐ Joshua 22—24
    ☐ Luke 3

27. ☐ Joshua 1—3
    ☐ Luke 4:1-30

28. ☐ Judges 4—6
    ☐ Luke 4:31-44

29. ☐ Judges 7—8
    ☐ Luke 5:1-16

30. ☐ Judges 9—10
    ☐ Luke 5:17-39

31. ☐ Judges 11—12
    ☐ Luke 6:1-26

April

1. ☐ Judges 13—15
   ☐ Luke 6:27-49

2. ☐ Judges 16—18
   ☐ Luke 7:1-30

3. ☐ Judges 19—21
   ☐ Luke 7:31-50

4. ☐ Ruth
   ☐ Luke 8:1-25

5. ☐ I Samuel 1—3
   ☐ Luke 8:26-56

6. ☐ I Samuel 4—6
   ☐ Luke 9:1-17

7. ☐ I Samuel 7—9
   ☐ Luke 9:18-36

8. ☐ I Samuel 10—12
   ☐ Luke 9:37-62

9. ☐ I Samuel 13—14
   ☐ Luke 10:1-24

10. ☐ I Samuel 15—16
    ☐ Luke 10:25-42

11. ☐ I Samuel 17—18
    ☐ Luke 11:1-28

12. ☐ I Samuel 19—21
    ☐ Luke 11:29-54

13. ☐ I Samuel 22—24
    ☐ Luke 12:1-31

14. ☐ I Samuel 25—26
    ☐ Luke 12:32-59

15. ☐ I Samuel 27—29
    ☐ Luke 13:1-22

16. ☐ I Samuel 30—31
    ☐ Luke 13:23-35

17. ☐ 2 Samuel 1—2
    ☐ Luke 14:1—24

18. ☐ 2 Samuel 3—5
    ☐ Luke 14:25-35

19. ☐ 2 Samuel 6—8
    ☐ Luke 15:1-10

20. ☐ 2 Samuel 9—11
    ☐ Luke 15:11-32

21. ☐ 2 Samuel 12—13
    ☐ Luke 16

22. ☐ 2 Samuel 14—15
    ☐ Luke 17:1-19

23. ☐ 2 Samuel 16—18
    ☐ Luke 17:20-37

24. ☐ 2 Samuel 19—20
    ☐ Luke 18:1-23

25. ☐ 2 Samuel 21—22
    ☐ Luke 18:24-43

26. ☐ 2 Samuel 23—24
    ☐ Luke 19:1-27

27. ☐ I Kings 1—2
    ☐ Luke 19:28-48

28. ☐ I Kings 3—5
    ☐ Luke 20:1-26

29. ☐ I Kings 6—7
    ☐ Luke 20:27-47

30. ☐ I Kings 8—9
    ☐ Luke 21:1-19

May

1. ☐ 1 Kings 10—11
   ☐ Luke 21:20-38

2. ☐ 1 Kings 12—13
   ☐ Luke 22:1-20

3. ☐ 1 Kings 14—15
   ☐ Luke 22:21-46

4. ☐ 1 Kings 16—18
   ☐ Luke 22:47-71

5. ☐ 1 Kings 19—20
   ☐ Luke 23:1-25

6. ☐ 1 Kings 21—22
   ☐ Luke 23:26-56

7. ☐ 2 Kings 1—3
   ☐ Luke 24:1-35

8. ☐ 2 Kings 4—6
   ☐ Luke 24:36-53

9. ☐ 2 Kings 7—9
   ☐ John 1:1-28

10. ☐ 2 Kings 10—12
    ☐ John 1:29-51

11. ☐ 2 Kings 13—14
    ☐ John 2

12. ☐ 2 Kings 15—16
    ☐ John 3:1-18

13. ☐ 2 Kings 17—18
    ☐ John 3:19-36

14. ☐ 2 Kings 19—21
    ☐ John 4:1-30

15. ☐ 2 Kings 22—23
    ☐ John 4:31-54

16. ☐ 2 Kings 24—25
    ☐ John 5:1-24

17. ☐ 1 Chronicles 1—3
    ☐ John 5:25-47

18. ☐ 1 Chronicles 4—6
    ☐ John 6:1-21

19. ☐ 1 Chronicles 7—9
    ☐ John 6:22-44

20. ☐ 1 Chronicles 10—12
    ☐ John 6:45-71

21. ☐ 1 Chronicles 13—15
    ☐ John 7:1-27

22. ☐ 1 Chronicles 16—18
    ☐ John 7:28-53

23. ☐ 1 Chronicles 19—21
    ☐ John 8:1-27

24. ☐ 1 Chronicles 22—24
    ☐ John 8:28-59

25. ☐ 1 Chronicles 25—27
    ☐ John 9:1-23

26. ☐ 1 Chronicles 28—29
    ☐ John 9:24-41

27. ☐ 2 Chronicles 1—3
    ☐ John 10:1-23

28. ☐ 2 Chronicles 4—6
    ☐ John 10:24-42

29. ☐ 2 Chronicles 7—9
    ☐ John 11:1-29

30. ☐ 2 Chronicles 10—12
    ☐ John 11:30-57

31. ☐ 2 Chronicles 13—14
    ☐ John 12:1-26

June

1. ☐ 2 Chronicles 15—16
   ☐ John 12:27-50

2. ☐ 2 Chronicles 17—18
   ☐ John 13:1-20

3. ☐ 2 Chronicles 19—20
   ☐ John 13:21-38

4. ☐ 2 Chronicles 21—22
   ☐ John 14

5. ☐ 2 Chronicles 23—24
   ☐ John 15

6. ☐ 2 Chronicles 25—27
   ☐ John 16

7. ☐ 2 Chronicles 28—29
   ☐ John 17

8. ☐ 2 Chronicles 30—31
   ☐ John 18:1-18

9. ☐ 2 Chronicles 32—33
   ☐ John 18:19-40

10. ☐ 2 Chronicles 34—36
    ☐ John 19:1-22

11. ☐ Ezra 1—2
    ☐ John 19:23-42

12. ☐ Ezra 3—5
    ☐ John 20

13. ☐ Ezra 6—8
    ☐ John 21

14. ☐ Ezra 9—10
    ☐ Acts 1

15. ☐ Nehemiah 1—3
    ☐ Acts 2:1-21

16. ☐ Nehemiah 4—6
    ☐ Acts 2:22-47

17. ☐ Nehemiah 7—9
    ☐ Acts 3

18. ☐ Nehemiah 10—11
    ☐ Acts 4:1-22

19. ☐ Nehemiah 12—13
    ☐ Acts 4:23-37

20. ☐ Esther 1—2
    ☐ Acts 5:1-21

21. ☐ Esther 3—5
    ☐ Acts 5:22-42

22. ☐ Esther 6—8
    ☐ Acts 6

23. ☐ Esther 9—10
    ☐ Acts 7:1-21

24. ☐ Job 1—2
    ☐ Acts 7:22-43

25. ☐ Job 3—4
    ☐ Acts 7:44-60

26. ☐ Job 5—7
    ☐ Acts 8:1-25

27. ☐ Job 8—10
    ☐ Acts 8:26-40

28. ☐ Job 11—13
    ☐ Acts 9:1-21

29. ☐ Job 14—16
    ☐ Acts 9:22-43

30. ☐ Job 17—19
    ☐ Acts 10:1-23

July

1. ☐ Job 20—21
   ☐ Acts 10:24-48

2. ☐ Job 22—24
   ☐ Acts 11

3. ☐ Job 25—27
   ☐ Acts 12

4. ☐ Job 28—29
   ☐ Acts 13:1-25

5. ☐ Job 30—31
   ☐ Acts 13:26-52

6. ☐ Job 32—33
   ☐ Acts 14

7. ☐ Job 34—35
   ☐ Acts 15:1-21

8. ☐ Job 36—37
   ☐ Acts 15:22-41

9. ☐ Job 38—40
   ☐ Acts 16:1-21

10. ☐ Job 41—42
    ☐ Acts 16:22-40

11. ☐ Psalm 1—3
    ☐ Acts 17:1-15

12. ☐ Psalm 4—6
    ☐ Acts 17:16-34

13. ☐ Psalm 7—9
    ☐ Acts 18

14. ☐ Psalm 10—12
    ☐ Acts 19:1-20

15. ☐ Psalm 13—15
    ☐ Acts 19:21-41

16. ☐ Psalm 16—17
    ☐ Acts 20:1-16

17. ☐ Psalm 18—19
    ☐ Acts 20:17-38

18. ☐ Psalm 20—22
    ☐ Acts 21:1-17

19. ☐ Psalm 23—25
    ☐ Acts 21:18-40

20. ☐ Psalm 26—28
    ☐ Acts 22

21. ☐ Psalm 29—30
    ☐ Acts 23:1-15

22. ☐ Psalm 31—32
    ☐ Acts 23:16-35

23. ☐ Psalm 33—34
    ☐ Acts 24

24. ☐ Psalm 35—36
    ☐ Acts 25

25. ☐ Psalm 37—39
    ☐ Acts 26

26. ☐ Psalm 40—42
    ☐ Acts 27:1-26

27. ☐ Psalm 43—45
    ☐ Acts 27:27-44

28. ☐ Psalm 46—48
    ☐ Acts 28

29. ☐ Psalm 49—50
    ☐ Romans 1

30. ☐ Psalm 51—53
    ☐ Romans 2

31. ☐ Psalm 54—56
    ☐ Romans 3

August

1. ☐ Psalm 57—59
   ☐ Romans 4

2. ☐ Psalm 60—62
   ☐ Romans 5

3. ☐ Psalm 63—65
   ☐ Romans 6

4. ☐ Psalm 66—67
   ☐ Romans 7

5. ☐ Psalm 68—69
   ☐ Romans 8:1-21

6. ☐ Psalm 70—71
   ☐ Romans 8:22-39

7. ☐ Psalm 72—73
   ☐ Romans 9:1-15

8. ☐ Psalm 74—76
   ☐ Romans 9:16-33

9. ☐ Psalm 77—78
   ☐ Romans 10

10. ☐ Psalm 79—80
    ☐ Romans 11:1-18

11. ☐ Psalm 81—83
    ☐ Romans 11:19-36

12. ☐ Psalm 84—86
    ☐ Romans 12

13. ☐ Psalm 87—88
    ☐ Romans 13

14. ☐ Psalm 89—90
    ☐ Romans 14

15. ☐ Psalm 91—93
    ☐ Romans 15:1-13

16. ☐ Psalm 94—96
    ☐ Romans 15:14-33

17. ☐ Psalm 97—99
    ☐ Romans 16

18. ☐ Psalm 100—102
    ☐ I Corinthians 1

19. ☐ Psalm 103—104
    ☐ 1 Corinthians 2

20. ☐ Psalm 105—106
    ☐ 1 Corinthians 3

21. ☐ Psalm 107—109
    ☐ 1 Corinthians 4

22. ☐ Psalm 110—112
    ☐ 1 Corinthians 5

23. ☐ Psalm 113—115
    ☐ 1 Corinthians 6

24. ☐ Psalm 116—118
    ☐ 1 Corinthians 7:1-19

25. ☐ Psalm 119:1-88
    ☐ 1 Corinthians 7:20-40

26. ☐ Psalm 119:89-176
    ☐ I Corinthians 8

27. ☐ Psalm 120—122
    ☐ I Corinthians 9

28. ☐ Psalm 123—125
    ☐ I Corinthians 10:1-18

29. ☐ Psalm 126—128
    ☐ I Corinthians 10:19-33

30. ☐ Psalm 129—131
    ☐ I Corinthians 11:1-16

31. ☐ Psalm 132—134
    ☐ I Corinthians 11:17-34

September

1. ☐ Psalm 135—136
   ☐ 1 Corinthians 12

2. ☐ Psalm 137—139
   ☐ I Corinthians 13

3. ☐ Psalm 140—142
   ☐ I Corinthians 14:1-20

4. ☐ Psalm 143—145
   ☐ I Corinthians 14:21-40

5. ☐ Psalm 146—147
   ☐ I Corinthians 15:1-28

6. ☐ Psalm 148—150
   ☐ 1 Corinthians 15:29-58

7. ☐ Proverbs 1—2
   ☐ 1 Corinthians 16

8. ☐ Proverbs 3—5
   ☐ 2 Corinthians 1

9. ☐ Proverbs 6—7
   ☐ 2 Corinthians 2

10. ☐ Proverbs 8—9
    ☐ 2 Corinthians 3

11. ☐ Proverbs 10—12
    ☐ 2 Corinthians 4

12. ☐ Proverbs 13—15
    ☐ 2 Corinthians 5

13. ☐ Proverbs 16—18
    ☐ 2 Corinthians 6

14. ☐ Proverbs 19—21
    ☐ 2 Corinthians 7

15. ☐ Proverbs 22—24
    ☐ 2 Corinthians 8

16. ☐ Proverbs 25—26
    ☐ 2 Corinthians 9

17. ☐ Proverbs 27—29
    ☐ 2 Corinthians 10

18. ☐ Proverbs 30—31
    ☐ 2 Corinthians 11:1-15

19. ☐ Ecclesiastes 1—3
    ☐ 2 Corinthians 11:16-33

20. ☐ Ecclesiastes 4—6
    ☐ 2 Corinthians 12

21. ☐ Ecclesiastes 7—9
    ☐ 2 Corinthians 13

22. ☐ Ecclesiastes 10—12
    ☐ Galatians 1

23. ☐ Song of Solomon 1—3
    ☐ Galatians 2

24. ☐ Song of Solomon 4—5
    ☐ Galatians 3

25. ☐ Song of Solomon 6—8
    ☐ Galatians 4

26. ☐ Isaiah 1—2
    ☐ Galatians 5

27. ☐ Isaiah 3—4
    ☐ Galatians 6

28. ☐ Isaiah 5—6
    ☐ Ephesians 1

29. ☐ Isaiah 7—8
    ☐ Ephesians 2

30. ☐ Isaiah 9—10
    ☐ Ephesians 3

October

1. ☐ Isaiah 11—13
   ☐ Ephesians 4

2. ☐ Isaiah 14—16
   ☐ Ephesians 5:1-16

3. ☐ Isaiah 17—19
   ☐ Ephesians 5:17-33

4. ☐ Isaiah 20—22
   ☐ Ephesians 6

5. ☐ Isaiah 23—25
   ☐ Philippians 1

6. ☐ Isaiah 26—27
   ☐ Philippians 2

7. ☐ Isaiah 28—29
   ☐ Philippians 3

8. ☐ Isaiah 30—31
   ☐ Philippians 4

9. ☐ Isaiah 32—33
   ☐ Colossians 1

10. ☐ Isaiah 34—36
    ☐ Colossians 2

11. ☐ Isaiah 37—38
    ☐ Colossians 3

12. ☐ Isaiah 39—40
    ☐ Colossians 4

13. ☐ Isaiah 41—42
    ☐ 1 Thessalonians 1

14. ☐ Isaiah 43—44
    ☐ 1 Thessalonians 2

15. ☐ Isaiah 45—46
    ☐ 1 Thessalonians 3

16. ☐ Isaiah 47—49
    ☐ 1 Thessalonians 4

17. ☐ Isaiah 50—52
    ☐ I Thessalonians 5

18. ☐ Isaiah 53—55
    ☐ 2 Thessalonians 1

19. ☐ Isaiah 56—58
    ☐ 2 Thessalonians 2

20. ☐ Isaiah 59—61
    ☐ 2 Thessalonians 3

21. ☐ Isaiah 62—64
    ☐ I Timothy 1

22. ☐ Isaiah 65—66
    ☐ I Timothy 2

23. ☐ Jeremiah 1—2
    ☐ I Timothy 3

24. ☐ Jeremiah 3—5
    ☐ I Timothy 4

25. ☐ Jeremiah 6—8
    ☐ I Timothy 5

26. ☐ Jeremiah 9—11
    ☐ I Timothy 6

27. ☐ Jeremiah 12—14
    ☐ 2 Timothy 1

28. ☐ Jeremiah 15—17
    ☐ 2 Timothy 2

29. ☐ Jeremiah 18—19
    ☐ 2 Timothy 3

30. ☐ Jeremiah 20—21
    ☐ 2 Timothy 4

31. ☐ Jeremiah 22—23
    ☐ Titus 1

November

1. ☐ Jeremiah 24—26
   ☐ Titus 2

2. ☐ Jeremiah 27—29
   ☐ Titus 3

3. ☐ Jeremiah 30—31
   ☐ Philemon

4. ☐ Jeremiah 32—33
   ☐ Hebrews 1

5. ☐ Jeremiah 34—36
   ☐ Hebrews 2

6. ☐ Jeremiah 37—39
   ☐ Hebrews 3

7. ☐ Jeremiah 40—42
   ☐ Hebrews 4

8. ☐ Jeremiah 43—45
   ☐ Hebrews 5

9. ☐ Jeremiah 46—47
   ☐ Hebrews 6

10. ☐ Jeremiah 48—49
    ☐ Hebrews 7

11. ☐ Jeremiah 50
    ☐ Hebrews 8

12. ☐ Jeremiah 51—52
    ☐ Hebrews 9

13. ☐ Lamentations 1—2
    ☐ Hebrews 10:1-18

14. ☐ Lamentations 3—5
    ☐ Hebrews 10:19-39

15. ☐ Ezekiel 1—2
    ☐ Hebrews 11:1-19

16. ☐ Ezekiel 3—4
    ☐ Hebrews 11:20-40

17. ☐ Ezekiel 5—7
    ☐ Hebrews 12

18. ☐ Ezekiel 8—10
    ☐ Hebrews 13

19. ☐ Ezekiel 11—13
    ☐ James 1

20. ☐ Ezekiel 14—15
    ☐ James 2

21. ☐ Ezekiel 16—17
    ☐ James 3

22. ☐ Ezekiel 18—19
    ☐ James 4

23. ☐ Ezekiel 20—21
    ☐ James 5

24. ☐ Ezekiel 22—23
    ☐ 1 Peter 1

25. ☐ Ezekiel 24—26
    ☐ I Peter 2

26. ☐ Ezekiel 27—29
    ☐ 1 Peter 3

27. ☐ Ezekiel 30—32
    ☐ 1 Peter 4

28. ☐ Ezekiel 33—34
    ☐ 1 Peter 5

29. ☐ Ezekiel 35—36
    ☐ 2 Peter 1

30. ☐ Ezekiel 37—39
    ☐ 2 Peter 2

December

1. ☐ Ezekiel 40—41
   ☐ 2 Peter 3

2. ☐ Ezekiel 42—44
   ☐ 1 John 1

3. ☐ Ezekiel 45—46
   ☐ 1 John 2

4. ☐ Ezekiel 47—48
   ☐ 1 John 3

5. ☐ Daniel 1—2
   ☐ I John 4

6. ☐ Daniel 3—4
   ☐ I John 5

7. ☐ Daniel 5—7
   ☐ 2 John

8. ☐ Daniel 8—10
   ☐ 3 John

9. ☐ Daniel 11—12
   ☐ Jude

10. ☐ Hosea 1—4
    ☐ Revelation 1

11. ☐ Hosea 5—8
    ☐ Revelation 2

12. ☐ Hosea 9—11
    ☐ Revelation 3

13. ☐ Hosea 12—14
    ☐ Revelation 4

14. ☐ Joel
    ☐ Revelation 5

15. ☐ Amos 1—3
    ☐ Revelation 6

16. ☐ Amos 4—6
    ☐ Revelation 7

17. ☐ Amos 7—9
    ☐ Revelation 8

18. ☐ Obadiah
    ☐ Revelation 9

19. ☐ Jonah
    ☐ Revelation 10

20. ☐ Micah 1—3
    ☐ Revelation 11

21. ☐ Micah 4—5
    ☐ Revelation 12

22. ☐ Micah 6—7
    ☐ Revelation 13

23. ☐ Nahum
    ☐ Revelation 14

24. ☐ Habakkuk
    ☐ Revelation 15

25. ☐ Zephaniah
    ☐ Revelation 16

26. ☐ Haggai
    ☐ Revelation 17

27. ☐ Zechariah 1—4
    ☐ Revelation 18

28. ☐ Zechariah 5—8
    ☐ Revelation 19

29. ☐ Zechariah 9—12
    ☐ Revelation 20

30. ☐ Zechariah 13—14
    ☐ Revelation 21

31. ☐ Malachi
    ☐ Revelation 22

Surge Protector Scriptures

The Bridge
(Plan of Salvation)

Surge Protectors

These are promises from God to you. Learn them. Believe them.

When you are tested and tempted, remember this!

No test or temptation that comes your way is beyond the course of what others have to face. All you need to remember is that God will never let you down; he'll never let you be pushed past your limit; he'll always be there to help you come through it.
      1 Corinthians 10:13 THE MESSAGE

Every part of Scripture is God-breathed and useful one way or another–showing us truth, exposing our rebellion, correcting our mistakes, training us to live God's way. Through the Word we are put together and shaped up for the tasks God has for us.
      2 Timothy 3:16-17 THE MESSAGE

Anyone who meets a testing challenge head-on and manages to stick it out is mighty fortunate. For such persons loyally in love with God, the reward is life and more life.
      James 1:12 THE MESSAGE

So let God work his will in you. Yell a loud *no* to the devil and watch him scamper. Say a quiet *yes* to God and he'll be there in no time.
      James 4:7 THE MESSAGE

When you're tired of trying and feeling weak, remember this!

My grace is enough; it's all you need. My strength comes into its own in your weakness.
      2 Corinthians 12:9 THE MESSAGE

Don't love the world's ways. Don't love the world's goods. Love of the world squeezes out love for the Father.
      1 John 2:15 THE MESSAGE

Look at me. I stand at the door. I knock. If you hear me call and open the door, I'll come right in and sit down to supper with you.
    Revelation 3:20 *The Message*

If any of you lacks wisdom, he should ask God, who gives generously to all without finding fault, and it will be given to him.
    James 1:5 (NIV)

Without faith it is impossible to please God, because anyone who comes to him must believe that he exists and that he rewards those who earnestly seek him.
    Hebrews 11:6 (NIV)

I press on toward the goal to win the prize for which God has called me.
    Philippians 3:14 (NIV)

He who began a good work in you will carry it on to completion until the day of Christ Jesus.
    Philippians 1:6 (NIV)

May the words of my mouth and the meditation of my heart be pleasing in your sight, O Lord.
    Psalm 19:14 (NIV)

Whatever you do, work at it with all your heart, as working for the Lord, not for men.
    Colossians 3:23 (NIV)

I will praise you because I am fearfully and wonderfully made.
    Psalm 139:14 (NIV)

"For I know the plans I have for you," declares the Lord, "plans to prosper you and not to harm you, plans to give you hope and a future."
    Jeremiah 29:11 (NIV)

I can do everything through him who gives me strength.
    Philippians 4:13 (NIV)

All things are possible with God.
        Mark 10:27 (NIV)

We know that in all things God works for the good of those who love him.
        Romans 8:28 (NIV)

Trust in the Lord with all your heart and lean not on your own understanding.
        Proverbs 3:5 (NIV)

He will command his angels concerning you to guard you in all your ways.
        Psalm 91:11 (NIV)

Seek first his kingdom and his righteousness, and all these things will be given to you as well.
        Matthew 6:33 (NIV)

Be strong and courageous. Do not be terrified; do not be discouraged, for the Lord your God will be with you wherever you go.
        Joshua 1:9 (NIV)

My help comes from the Lord, the Maker of heaven and earth.
        Psalm 121:2 (NIV)

Give thanks in all circumstances, for this is God's will for you in Christ Jesus.
        1 Thessalonians 5:18 (NIV)

Your word is a lamp to my feet and a light for my path.
        Psalm 119:105 (NIV)

For you have been my hope, O Sovereign Lord, my confidence.
        Psalm 71:5 (NIV)

Do to others what you would have them do to you.
        Matthew 7:12 (NIV)

This is the day the Lord has made; let us rejoice and be glad in it.
    Psalm 118:24 (NIV)

Ask and it will be given to you; seek and you will find; knock and the door will be opened to you.
    Matthew 7:7 (NIV)

I have hidden your word in my heart that I might not sin against you.
    Psalm 119:11 (NIV)

My command is this: Love each other as I have loved you.
    John 15:12 (NIV)

For God so love the world that he gave his one and only Son, that whoever believes in him shall not perish but have eternal life.
    John 3:16 (NIV)

Live a life of love, just as Christ loved us.
    Ephesians 5:2 (NIV)

Cast all your anxiety on him because he cares for you.
    1 Peter 5:7 (NIV)

Do not be anxious about anything, but in everything, by prayer and petition, with thanksgiving, present your requests to God.
    Philippians 4:6 (NIV)

If we love one another, God lives in us and his love is made complete in us.
    1 John 4:12 (NIV)

In all your ways acknowledge Him, and He will make your paths straight.
    Proverbs 3:6 (NIV)

The Lord is my shepherd, I shall not be in want.
    Psalm 23:1 (NIV)

Those who hope in the Lord will renew their strength.
    Isaiah 40:31 (NIV)

Be strong and courageous. Do not be afraid or terrified…
the Lord your God goes with you; he will never leave you nor forsake you.
> Deuteronomy 31:6 (NIV)

The Lord is my light and my salvation—whom shall I fear?
> Psalm 27:1 (NIV)

I sought the Lord, and he answered me; he delivered me from all my fears.
> Psalm 34:4 (NIV)

Keep your tongue from evil and your lips from speaking lies.
> Psalm 34:13 (NIV)

Turn from evil and do good; seek peace and pursue it.
> Psalm 34:14 (NIV)

Delight yourself in the Lord and he will give you the desires of your heart.
> Psalm 37:4 (NIV)

God is our refuge and strength, an ever-present help in trouble.
> Psalm 46:1 (NIV)

A gentle answer turns away wrath, but a harsh word stirs up anger.
> Proverbs 15:1 (NIV)

You will seek me and find me when you seek me with all your heart.
> Jeremiah 29:13 (NIV)

Call to me and I will answer you and tell you great and unsearchable things you do not know.
> Jeremiah 33:3 (NIV)

What good will it be for a man if he gains the whole world, yet forfeits his soul?
> Matthew 16:26 (NIV)

The Bridge
Plan of Salvation

1. God's Plan

a. God created us; He loves us, and wants to have a relationship with us.

b. 1 John 4:10 – God...loved us and sent his Son as a sacrifice to clear away our sins and the damage they've done to our relationship with God.

2. Our Problem

a. Everyone has done wrong and disobeyed God—that breaks our relationship with Him—causes a BIG GAP between us and God.

b. Romans 3:23 – We've compiled this long and sorry record as sinners...and proved that we are utterly incapable of living the glorious lives God wants for us.

c. This gap makes God sad because He loves us so much!

d. Sometimes we try to do things to get back to God, but they don't work.

e. Proverbs 14:12 – There's a way of life that looks harmless enough; look again—it leads straight to hell.

3. God's Cure

a. God did for us what we couldn't do. He sent Jesus to die for us on the cross.

b. Romans 5:8 – But God put his love on the line for us by offering his Son in sacrificial death while we were of no use whatever to him.

c. The cross bridges the gap between us and God.

4. Our Choice

a. It's not enough just to know this, we have to act on it by admitting that we have sinned by disobeying; that we want His forgiveness, and that we'll trust Him with our lives!

b. John 5:24 – Anyone here who believes what I am saying... and aligns himself with the Father...has at this very moment the real, lasting life and is no longer condemned to be an outsider. This person has taken a giant step from the world of the dead to the world of the living.

c. Does this make sense to you? Are you ready?

In plain English...do the following:

- Admit you've done wrong (I have sinned)
- Ask God to forgive you and to help you change your behavior (repent)
- Believe!—Jesus died on the cross for you and rose from the grave
- Invite Jesus to live in and through you

This will help...

- Read your Bible every day
- Talk to Jesus every day in prayer
- Tell others about Jesus
- Worship with other Christians
- Show Jesus to others by the way you care for them, talk to them, and serve them

notes:

Notes:

notes:

notes: